Yoruba and Ifá

Unlocking the Secrets of Orishas, Isese, Divination, Santeria, and More

Your Free Gift
(only available for a limited time)

Thanks for getting this book! If you want to learn more about various spirituality topics, then join Mari Silva's community and get a free guided meditation MP3 for awakening your third eye. This guided meditation mp3 is designed to open and strengthen ones third eye so you can experience a higher state of consciousness. Simply visit the link below the image to get started.

https://spiritualityspot.com/meditation

Table of Contents

Part 1: Yoruba

The Ultimate Guide to Ifa Spirituality, Isese, Odu, Orishas, Santeria, and More

THE ULTIMATE GUIDE TO IFA
SPIRITUALITY, ISESE, ODU,
ORISHAS, SANTERIA, AND MORE

MARI SILVA

Introduction

The Yoruba traditional religion has grown in popularity over the past few decades, especially among African-Americans, as this spiritual Ifa system provides a profound sense of cultural belonging. Yoruba is a fascinating tradition made up of myths, lore, legends, indigenous beliefs, traditional songs, and folk proverbs, which are all shaped by the social and cultural contexts of West Africa.

This book serves as the ultimate guide on Ifa spirituality, Isese, Odu, Orishas, Santeria, and more. In it, you'll find in-depth illustrations of the Yoruba tradition, exploring all its elements and influence, and it covers a wide area of one of the most popular and complex of the West African belief system. Learning everything there is to know about this belief system is not something that you can do overnight, especially since there are many terms and cultural contexts people may find very unfamiliar. Fortunately, this book presents the topic in an interesting, easy-to-understand manner. Despite being easy to follow the guide, the book delves deeply into salient topics, ensuring that all the aspects of this spiritual system are covered. This makes it ideal for beginners who have no background in the Yoruba and more experienced individuals who wish to refine and enrich their knowledge.

In this book, you'll find hands-on instructions and methods when it comes to creating an ancestral altar, honoring the ancestors, and making offerings to them, as well as making Yoruba spells, rituals, and baths.

The book provides a thorough introduction to the Yoruba and a brief historical and cultural background. You'll understand how religion didn't wither with the passage of time and remained strong in the face of historical difficulties. You'll also better understand the main Yoruba beliefs and worldview. Then, the book will illustrate insightful details on the Supreme Yoruba God, Olorun, and the creation myth. You'll learn about the creation story and understand how the Yoruba Supreme God manifests himself in three ways.

As you read, you'll be learning about the Irunmole and Orishas and how they can help you, and understand the importance of offerings and how each Orisha has a preferred offering. The book will lead you through the sacred feminine and masculine concepts in Yoruba and present the appropriate deities, along with their origin stories, colors, personalities, and how they were typically worshiped. The following chapter then uncovers the Ifa divination practice and explains who can be an Ifa priest. The book will also walk you through a description of the Yoruba worship calendar and its holy days and how the Yoruba religion managed to influence other African diaspora religions. Finally, you'll find an Orisha offering cheat sheet that you can refer to whenever you need to be reminded of the Orishas and their preferred offerings.

Chapter 1: Introduction to Yoruba

African traditional society, which includes the Yoruba belief system, covers indigenous spiritual concepts and religions of the African population which are not Christian or Islamic. It encompasses a wide array of ritualistic practices, symbols, artistic expressions, customary practices, cosmology, culture, society, etc. If you're a spiritual person, then the chances are that you think of religion as a lifestyle. This is why it only makes sense that African traditional religion and all its elements would have influenced the worldview of the African population.

As opposed to what many people may think, traditional African belief systems are dynamic. They are dynamic and are highly reactive to everything that causes a shift in concepts and ideologies, like aging, technological advances, and the passage of time. These traditional religions are also mostly concerned with life experiences – instead of being doctrine and faith-oriented, they incorporate a multitude of ceremonies, rituals, and other hands-on practices; this makes them incredibly relatable and tangible to those who practice them.

The Triple Heritage

If you read about African religions, you may have noticed that academics usually bring up *triple heritage*. This is because African societies are typically a blend of Christianity, Islam, and indigenous belief systems, which are the *triple legacy*. You may even be surprised to know that even though the people who practice traditional African religion are considered a minority, Christians and Muslims who live in the region are involved in the practices of traditional religions in one way or another. The traditional belief system still influences various aspects of African societies, including its political, social, and economic facets. However, a large portion of the population has converted to Christianity and Islam.

Unlike Christianity and Islam, which are concerned with garnering conversions, traditional African tradition is driven by co-existence. One of its pillars is to encourage peace and harmonious interactions. They encourage the maintenance of good relationships with followers of other beliefs and practitioners of different spiritual activities. While Islam and Christianity still promote the tolerance of all, the followers of traditional African religions don't feel the need to encourage others to adopt their beliefs.

The Influence of Traditional African Beliefs

Few people are aware that these religions have traveled far beyond the borders of their home continent. This diffusion happened during the Trans-Atlantic slave trade and has inspired the emergence of other traditions and belief systems in the Americas, such as the Vodun in Haïti, Santería in Cuba, and Candomblé in Brazil. The relationship and similarities between Yoruba and other religions, including the ones we had just mentioned, will be explored in more depth in the last chapter. African traditional religions' relevance and global reach made these beliefs very attractive to people on diasporic pilgrimages to the continent.

In essence, African religions are particularly interested in reproduction, wealth, and health. This heightened concern is what set off the establishment of institutions and organizations made especially for matters like commerce, healing, and the promotion of the general well-being of the advocates and practitioners of African religions and the members of other religious groups.

Society, Gender, and the Environment

While traditional African religions have set the tone for solid discussions regarding civil religion and society and community interactions, many people still believe that these beliefs conflict with modernity. Unfortunately, this has made minority groups, or the followers of this tradition, subject to inhumane forms of abuse.

Women figure very prominently in these belief systems, which strongly emphasize gender dynamics and relations by highlighting female deities and, to a lesser extent, their divine male counterparts. Goddesses, priestesses, diviners, and other female archetypes are eminent in myths and tales. Modern-day feminist academics even refer to these traditions in their efforts to advocate for the rights of women and their role in African societies. Indigenous African tradition approaches gender in the sense that one is complementary to the other. The forces of the feminine and the masculine must work in tandem.

Another very significant issue is that traditional African tradition discusses our interaction with the environment. These beliefs show a great deal of insight and discernment into how we can live in our environment without causing any harm. This is a topic of great importance in today's world, considering the imminent ecological crisis.

Spirituality and Tradition

Traditional African religions offer robust associations between the realm of ancestors and the world of physical existence. This allows practitioners to keep in constant touch and maintain their relationships with their ancestors. According to indigenous beliefs, our ancestors are highly involved and intricately concerned with our daily life affairs.

Many religions in different parts of the world remain alive through their written texts and recorded scriptures. However, traditional African religion mainly relies on oral story-telling. These tales and oral sources have been elaborately integrated into the social and political structures, various forms of art, and other tangible aspects of culture. Since these traditions are essentially oral, they have left a window for variation and versatility used by various subgroups and multiple other African religions. The Yoruba Ifa tradition and other forms of orature still serve as significant sources of reference when it comes to understanding the religion's practices and its members' worldview.

Reading this chapter will help you understand what Yoruba, a traditional African religion, is. We uncover and try to explain the highly controversial origins and history of this traditional religion – the main Yoruba beliefs and worldviews and how it remained strong in the face of discrimination and disparagement from mainstream religions and societies throughout history.

The Yoruba in a Nutshell

West Africa is home to a group of ethnic peoples known as the Yoruba. As of 2019, there were approximately 44 million Yoruba people, most of whom settled in Nigeria and account for 21% of the nation's population. The Yoruba are among Africa's largest ethnic groups. They have their own language, Yoruba, and occupy other regions and countries besides Nigeria. This includes, but isn't limited to, Ghana, Dominican Republic, Cuba, Jamaica, Saint Lucia, Ivory Coast, Liberia, Venezuela, Brazil, Granada, Sierra Leone, Trinidad and Tobago, and Puerto Rico.

The traditions, spiritual ideologies, and customary practices have all evolved into one solid religious belief system. According to the Yoruba religions, all humans must experience *Ayanmo,* which can be translated into *fate* or *destiny.* This is why this traditional religion suggests that humans will inevitably unite with the divine, the creator and source of all existing energy, in spirit. This state of oneness is called *Olodumare.* Our thoughts, feelings, and actions are translated into interactions with other living entities in the physical realm. Our communications are all efforts to find and attain a destiny in the spiritual world. The followers of the Yoruba traditional religion believe that people who stop experiencing spiritual growth in any of the facets of their lives are bound for *Orun-Apadi,* which is the invisible world of potsherds. The Yoruba religion considers life and death as an endless cycle of existence. Its followers believe that humans constantly reappear in the form of a different physical entity as their spirits gradually develop toward transcendence.

According to the Yoruba belief system, people's destinies are predetermined before they are even born. Their homes, families, partners, career, interests, and even the time and cause of death are all determined beforehand. Followers of the Yoruba tradition believe that a person's plans, destiny, and promises are all forgotten at birth. However, it is also believed that we spend a lot of time and effort trying to remember these things and strive for the future that was destined for us. The Yoruba believers consider god to be the most powerful being and a supreme deity who is not bound by gender. God, or Olodumare, is thought to be living in the skies. Intercessors or Orishas would complete all communications between the Yoruba believers and God.

History and Origins

Ìṣẹ̀ṣẹ is the Yoruba traditional religion name in the Yoruba language. The word Ìṣẹ̀ṣẹ refers to the rituals, customs, and traditions that are widely practiced in the Yoruba cultural scene. This world is a contraction of two words: *Ìṣẹ̀* and *ìṣe.* The former can be translated into origin or source, and the latter means tradition or practice. When combined, the words mean *the source of our tradition.* This word was coined to signify the Yoruba belief system because the numerous traditions, practices, observations, concepts, and beliefs are all derived from the spiritual worship of the orisa or orisha. An orisha is a being that withholds the ability to reflect some of Olodumare's manifestations.

Yoruba Traditional Religion

Around 12 to 15 million Yoruba people live in southwest Nigeria, Togo, and the Republic of Benin, which was previously known as Dahomey. These individuals are considered to be the successors of one of the earliest and most prominent West African cultural traditions and belief systems. Linguistic experts and archeological evidence suggest these people have occupied their present-day geographic location since the 15th century BCE, at the very least. Like every other language, regional dialects for the Yoruba language have developed, signifying the urbanization and the distinction between Yoruba subgroups. These differences led to the emergence of a social system in the first millennium BCE. This structure was unique to the Sub-Saharan African population. The traditional home of the Yoruba was thriving by the 9th century BCE. Terracotta and bronze sculptures, which are now among the eloquent riches of Africa, were avidly created by artists over the next five centuries.

Yoruba mythology, oral tradition, and story-telling signify Odudwa, also called Odua, as the founder and first king of the Yoruba people. Some mythologies claim that the traditional home of Yoruba is the cradle of creation and that Odudwa is the god of all creation. However, oral tradition and tales insist that the lore surrounding Odudwa's possession of the throne hints at the conquest led by the people of the east, before the 19th century, of the Yoruba home. Odudwa's followers came up with an urban tradition and increased the archetype or prominence of the king, even though there was a very robust sociopolitical structure of a town under the administration of a king or chief among the subgroups of Yoruba. Later on, those who wished to assert their political validity had to present evidence of their decent or relation to Odudwa, even if they were immigrants. Those individuals were named the *sons of Odudwa*. They wore *adenla* or beaded crowns. It was said that these crowns were presented to them by Odudwa himself to serve as a representation of their sanctified power.

A Controversial Origin

For years there has been controversy surrounding the ethnogenesis of the Yoruba as both a culture and religion. Numerous historians have studied models to try to determine the origin of the Yoruba population. Much evidence leads back to ancient Egypt. However, it is worth noting that many schools of thought disagree when it comes to the historical analysis of the Yoruba and its traditions. While some historians strongly believe Egypt was the motherland of the Yoruba, others insist that the existence of Arabs and white-skinned Egyptians contradicts the belief that the Yoruba was birthed in Egypt.

It is believed that a source known as the *Ifa Corpus* is a chronicle of all mysteries associated with the presence of the Yoruba people. According to the source, the Yoruba people believe that the supreme God, or the Olodumare, is the creator of the universe and all other deities. Then, Oldumare and the other gods, including Orishanla, the arch-god who was greatly involved in the process, created humans. This is why it's believed that all human civilizations originated in the home of the Yoruba, which is traditionally known as *Ile Ife*. However, various Yoruba ethnogenesis religion-cultural records don't encompass the elements of modern historical methodology. This means that it lacks accurate dating, the pursuit of historical validity and truth, reliable sources, external proof, and structure. This is why it's likely that the information presented by the *Ifa Corpus* is no more than mere lore and mythology.

Even though the different schools of thought affect historical traditions, a very popular trend among modern historians is the heightened interest in the relationship between the Yoruba and ancient Egypt. As we mentioned, it has become a very popular claim that the Yoruba peoples migrated from Egypt. They claim there is evidence of a religious and cultural link between the ancient Egyptians and the Yoruba. However, aside from the argument regarding the white-skinned Egyptians and the Arabs, many scholars insist there's no solid archeological evidence of the migration of the Egyptians to the land of the Yoruba. If either population had interacted with the other, then, according to historians, it would've likely occurred during the predynastic and dynastic eras, which explains the potential influences.

Additionally, numerous factors may have contributed to the belief that there was direct contact between ancient Egyptians and the Yoruba. This includes colonialism, Islam, Christianity, the Yoruba Creation myth, and the belief that Egypt is the motherland of all human civilization which we will discuss in more depth in the following chapters.

Maintaining Strength

As we mentioned at the beginning of the chapter, practitioners of traditional African religion have been subject to harsh forms of abuse. This is because of the alarmingly dangerous extremism and conflicts associated with Abrahamic monotheistic religions, like Judaism, Christianity, and Islam. These dangers are present within the borders of the African continent and are a looming threat to the practitioners of this religion all around the globe. This terrifying and unjust trend has affected Indigenous southwestern Nigerian Yoruba peoples. Christianity and Islam have unjustly intruded into the lives of the Yoruba peoples, causing turbulence and triggering spiritual imbalance among the traditional religion practitioners. The followers of Abrahamic religions have often conducted waves of forced conversions and actively spoken hatefully toward the believers of other faiths. They treated them as inferior and exposed them to other forms of abuse and prejudice, introducing malevolent characteristics into the society of the Yoruba.

The unwelcome arrival of the spiritual differences into the Yoruba society stimulated religious conflict, but it also led to the onset of superfluous homicide. This was a highly unfamiliar and confusing series of events to the Yoruba, considering their beliefs are fundamentally built on cordial concepts and characteristics like acceptance, harmony, tolerance, and co-existence. The practitioners of that faith are never focused on converting others to their religion or making sure that those around them share the same ideologies and concepts. The extreme efforts to convert members of the Yoruba religious groups rippled disruption, confusion, and feelings of anger and hurt among members of the society. However, the followers of this belief system seem to have managed to stay resilient regardless of the unpleasant disruption.

Another challenge that has acted as a threat to the Yoruba belief system is modernization and rapid technological advancements. All traditions and customs are at a constant threat of disappearance or alteration with the fast-paced nature of today's world. Traditions are typically replaced, forgotten, or entirely lost over time. Fortunately, the West African Yoruba peoples have maintained and kept a strong grip on their traditions. The Yoruba is among the few religious practices and traditions that stay very similar to how it was practiced centuries ago. The Yoruba people have done an excellent job at maintaining their truth.

Lukumi, one of the Yoruba dialects, is the liturgical language of numerous divisions of the subgroups that emerged of the Vodun, Santeria, and Candomble traditions. Nigeria was home to all of these religions. However, they were soon forcefully amalgamated with Catholicism at the start of the slave trade. Slaves were forced to adopt Christianity by their owners and the missionaries. However, their shipment destination was what determined their religious journey and spiritual beliefs. For instance, the slaves that ended up in South America were determined to keep practicing their Yoruba traditions. These traditions were inevitably blended with Catholicism to form Candomble. Spanish-owned slaves, on the other hand, who ended up in Spain founded Santeria. Lastly, the slaves who found themselves in France created Vodun. The point behind incorporating their current beliefs into their forced practices was to endure survival and maintenance of African beliefs and traditions. It was also a means of protection, as the Yoruba would be subject to harsh and severe abuse or punishment if they were found practicing their traditional religion. In response, they disguised their deities as Catholic saints and continued to worship them. They found saints whose characteristics most resembled their gods and assigned them to the corresponding Yoruba deity. This way, it would look like they were honoring catholic archetypes and celebrating Christian feasts when in reality, they were being loyal to their deities or Orisha. For instance, the Christian equivalent of Shango, the Yoruba king, is St. Barbara. This meant that conducting a drum party for St. Barbara was, in reality, one for Shango.

The determination to keep the Yoruba traditional religious beliefs alive – despite the endless challenges – ensured that we have the information available. Otherwise, the chances are that little would've been known about this belief system today. This is especially true for a religion primarily relying on oral story-telling and tradition.

The Yoruba religious tradition is among the most prominent indigenous African belief systems. This religion is highly versatile and adaptable. It also provides a great deal of insight and wisdom into topics of great importance, even to this day. This is perhaps why it is very relatable and appealing. Despite its complex and controversial history and the multitude of challenges it has faced, this religion has managed to thrive.

Chapter 2: Olorun and the Creation Myth

As you have read in the previous chapter, Yoruba beliefs represent a unique worldview based on spirituality and ancient traditions. This chapter will discuss one of these remarkable views – the relation between the Supreme Yoruba God, Olorun, and the Yoruba creation myth. This religion has its own creation story that's very different from those of other religions past and present. This tale transcended many generations through oral tradition, and the story of creation changed very little and remained faithful to traditions honoring Olorun and the Orishas. It also provides great insight into how the Yoruba see their Supreme God and their relationship with other supernatural beings and mortals.

The Yoruba Creation Myth

Eons ago, when mortals did not yet exist, Olorun and the Orishas lived in the sky – the only livable place at the time. Below them, there was only water, ruled by the goddess Olokun – ruler of the sea. Since the Orishas weren't as powerful as the Supreme God and often needed guidance, they all lived in a close community near a baobab tree. Here everyone found everything they needed to have a happy and peaceful existence. Despite having powers to do much more than that, they lived almost as mortals, tending to their daily needs. The Orishas created everything for their sustenance to pass their days, including stunning clothes and jewelry. They even had had the entire sky reaching above their heads had they wished to see more of their world. However, not everyone was satisfied with their blissful life in their community or wanted to see only the misty sky. Obatala was an Orisha who possessed great powers and an even larger desire to use them to explore far beyond their ruler's land and create something different. Soon, he started wondering what he could do with them, and while doing so, he suddenly looked down and noticed the waters below. It was then that Obatala realized where to begin his new adventure – and he immediately went to Olorun for permission to build something in the water. He had two reasons for this. Firstly, he needed to create a solid ground on which Obatala himself could stand when he ascended. Secondly, he wanted to make a land for new creatures – someone whom the Orishas could help, so they could finally use their great powers. Seeing that Obatala wanted to do something good and constructive for all of them, Olorun permitted him to descend onto the land of water.

Obatala then consulted another Orisha, Orunmila, about preparing for the journey. Orunmila is said to have divination powers, so he could see everything Obatala may need to make his future quest successful. He conducted a divination ritual by sprinkling powder made of baobab tree roots on a sacred tray. After tossing 16 palm kernels on the tray, Orunmila carefully observed the pattern they left while traveling on the tray. He repeated the process eight times, each time memorizing the kernel markings. His instruction to Obatala was to collect some baobab seeds, maize, sand, and palm nuts to sow and a black cat for company. In addition, Orunimla said to Obatala that the only way to reach the waters was to climb down on a golden chain. He also instructed Obatala to collect personal items from the other Orishas and place them in a sacred egg. At first, Obatala was concerned about finding a gold chain long enough to reach all the way to the world beneath his. He had an idea to go to all the Orishas and ask for their golden jewelry, which he could melt into a chain. He took all the gold given to him to an Orisha known to have exceptional metalsmithing skills. This smith then created a chain long enough to safely help Obatala reach the waters. The chain also had several powerful hooks, so Obatala could secure himself and the items he was carrying with him.

While the smith was making the chain, Obatala went on to find a seashell in which he could gather sand. He then put the cat, the baobab powder mixed with sand, and the maize into the bag and went to look around to find palm nuts and any other seeds he could take with him into this new land. When he gathered everything, Obatala secured the egg to his body with a piece of cloth, ensuring its protection during his climb.

After this, Obatala took the bag with the rest of the items and was almost ready for his journey. His last task was to secure one end of the chain to post in the skies, so he'll be able to climb it safely.

After seven days and nights, his journey came to a sudden halt when he ran out of chain. However, the chain didn't reach the waters yet, so Obatala didn't know how to get lower to the watery kingdom. As he wondered what he should do next, he heard Orunmila calling to him to take the sand from the bag and begin pouring it below him. As soon as he started to spill the sand onto the water, to his surprise, it solidified instantly, creating a firm ground on which he could walk. Unbeknown to him, Obatala had made the egg so warm with his worrying that the spiritual possessions inside it turned into a bird ready to hatch. When it did, a bird named Sankofa flew from it, carrying the spirits of the Orishas. Landing on the solid ground, the bird immediately started to peck at the sand, and the Orisha spirits began to shape the land into mountains and valleys. This is how all these formations got their unique character – they inherited them from the Orishas spirits themselves.

Obatala finally unhooked himself from the chain and let himself drop to the ground when there was land as far as he could see. He decided to name this new land "Ife," which can be translated as the area separating the waters. Eager to explore this new land, Obatala started to walk while shaking his bag and scattering everything from it to the ground. As he did so, the seeds he had in it landed in the soil, and they soon began to grow. In fact, they were growing so fast that they turned everything green without

Obatala even seeing this at first. After walking for a long time, he finally turned around and saw palm trees that were already multiplying in his wake.

Obatala had the cat for company, but he still needed to pass his time somehow, so he started to explore what he could make from the palm trees and the other plants growing on Ife. He made wine from the palm trees, but he was bored drinking it alone. One time, while enjoying the wine and fashioning small clay figures, he got the idea to create creatures he could guide and who could also keep him company. The clay figures were not perfect, and he still didn't know how to shape them, so he consulted Orunmila and Olorun. They have decided that the imperfections didn't matter, but the creatures should be shaped resembling the Orishas and not the Supreme Being. It is believed it was Olofi, who suggested this, saying the world needed more Orishas, but there could only be one God. After all, it's the Orishas who deal with nature and living things. As the number of living things multiplied in Ife, there should have been more guides to watch over them. However, not wanting to grant them the same privileges as the creatures living in the sky, Olorun decided to make these new creatures mortal rather than immortal like the Orishas were.

In addition to their physical differences, Orunmila also suggested that the new creatures have different essences. He said some should be better than others, but none should be perfect inside or out. This way, they could learn from their own errors and the mistakes made by others. Although they were to be supervised by the Orishas, the new species should be able to create and keep the balance in nature and amongst their own communities. In addition to this, this new species should know hunger and desire – none of which were familiar to Orishas. Given the enormity of the tasks he has been given, Olorun encouraged Obatala to plant more plants and sculpt other creatures, such as fish, insects, and other animals, before his ultimate goal – humans. All the other creatures could serve mankind as food, and while he was doing this, he would have more time to learn how to create a more physically, intellectually, and spiritually evolved species. Olorun also warned Obatala that humans would also need to have a lengthy period of development to achieve their full potential. Unlike the other species – which may mature in weeks or months – humans will require years of development to learn values such as kindness, sacrifice, and balance.

After some time, curious about what's happening below, Olorun sent another Orisha to see how Obatala was fairing. The report he received said that while Obatala made figures for his entertainment, he still wished they would come to life. He wanted to see them prosper and guide them along their journey. To remedy this, Olorun directed an enormous fireball he made from the explosive gases of the sky to Ife. Not only did this fire help create more habitable land, but it also baked the forms created by Obata. Finally, Olorun sparked life into all the different shapes across Ife using his own powerful breath. After witnessing Obatala's joy with this new life, Olorun sent the fireball back to the sky, where it became the Sun. Realizing Obatala would need help with his task in the future, Olorun sent a couple more powerful Orishas, including Orunmila, to him.

So, Obatala and the other Orishas were doing this grueling work, and they were progressing nicely – at least until it came the time to sculpt the physical shapes of the humans. As Obatala strolled around contemplating how to shape them into the likeness of the Orishas, he got tired and stopped to rest. As he happened to be beside a clear pond, he decided to drink from it. But before actually tasting the water, he noticed his own face – the reflection of an Orisha. Finally, having an idea of what the new forms of life should look like, he immediately started to create them from the bits of clay he found at the side of the pond. Obatala was quite pleased with the end result and made many more clay bodies. He grew thirsty again a couple of times during his work – but he didn't always drink water. Sometimes, he would reach for the wine to quench his thirst, and soon he was quite intoxicated. As a result, the clay forms started to look more and more different, and some ended up missing limbs and other body parts. However, at the time, he didn't notice this, thinking that all his sculptures were beautiful. Besides, he was told the more different they look, the better. That being said, the next time he repeated the process, he did it without drinking wine, so he could focus more on forming them as wholesomely as he could.

Finally, when all the creatures came to life, Olorun descended on the chain as Olofi to see the images of all the living beings. Seeing the vast number of new species, Olofi decided to give each Orisha several of them to guide. Meanwhile, humans were given the task of watching over their natural environment. They were encouraged to report to the Orishas if anything needed changing, although they weren't taught how to communicate their needs. Orunmila created several paths for each human, while others empowered them with different qualities, shaping their final destiny.

Initially curious about the new life evolving around her water kingdom, Olokun didn't interfere with the work of the Orishas. However, seeing how much the new species usurped her domain, she grew angry and decided to take revenge. Taking advantage of the absence of Obatala while he was in his homeland, Olokun commanded her waters to swallow the solid land created by Obatala. The plants, the animals, and many humans died, and only a few people who thought to flee to the highest grounds and ask for help remained alive. They sought refuge and means to survive from Eshu, the only Orisha close by to help. Eshu also agreed to report what was happening to Olorun, but only after the humans offered a sacrifice to both him and Obatala. When Olorun heard what was happening in Ife, he immediately sent Orunmila down again, instructing him to cast spells to make the water retreat. Seeing the drylands reappear again, the human was very grateful to the Orishas and the Supreme God.

However, Olorun decided to empower them even more, seeing that mankind was developing much slower than expected and still could not survive on its own, let alone guard its natural surroundings. He asked Obatala to make them stronger physically and give them larger organs, including brains. Under the tutelage of the Orishas, this newer human species has become more resilient and aware of its surroundings. In addition, the humans were trained how to communicate with their Orishas. They learned which offerings and prayers to make to which Orisha and how to appease them should they make a mishap and disappoint the Orishas or Olorun. Those who weren't taught this yet were under Obatala's patronage, along with all the deformed creatures.

Olorun, Olofi, Olodumare, and the Orishas

While there was now a way for humans to convey messages to the Orishas, they could not do the same with the Supreme God. As the owner of the skies and everything below it, the Supreme God sat at the top of the Yoruba pantheon hierarchy. This ranking was maintained by the three representations of this Supreme God – Olorun, Olofi, and Olodumare.

Olodumare, the almighty, was the maker of the lands – and possibly the creator of the entire universe. However, this being never manifests or receives messages, not even via the Orishas. Its only purpose was to oversee its masterpiece.

Olorun was the only manifestation people could perceive and was always present in the sky, like the Sun. This representation helped maintain the natural order of things and enabled humans to enjoy the world Olodumare created. Apart from owning Orun, the land of spirits, Olorun also communicated with the Orishas but only if necessary.

On the other hand, Olofi was always at the disposal of the Orishas and allowed them to convey messages to and from people.

The Orishas also used this manifestation of the Supreme God as an aid in learning everything they needed to communicate with the people. Thanks to this manifestation, the Orishas could teach them to be more respectful towards others and themselves. It helped them understand how to maintain themselves healthy mentally and physically.

In addition, there are quite a few differences between Olorun and the rest of the Yoruba pantheon. For starters, unlike the Orishas, who can be both male and female, Olorun transcends both genders and is seen as a gender-neutral being. Olorun, as the Supreme Being, rules above everything and everyone else. The Orishas are only assistants, acting as the intermediaries between the Olorun and other beings. Yet, at the same time, for humans, Orishas are just as fundamental as the Supreme God itself. Olorun's energy flows through other Orishas and can't be reached directly.

Yoruba Proverbs and the Significance of Olorun

Ta ní tó Olórum? Edá tá mòla ò sí.

Who is as great as God? No human being knows tomorrow.

This illustrates that no one is more knowledgeable than Olorun. No one knows what destiny holds for them; only Olorun does. So before acting impulsively, it's always worth considering several possible outcomes of your actions. You'll avoid getting into unnecessary trouble.

Eni tí a ò lè mú, Olórum là ńfi lé lówó.

An adversary over whom one cannot prevail, one leaves for God's judgment.

It means that if an adversary is stronger than you, you should let God rule over them. Even if you meet someone causing you great harm, it's best to leave them in God's hands. Olorun will know how to deal with them and will always impart the punishment they deserve.

Olórum ìbá dá kan-in-kan-in tóbi tó esinsin, àtapa ni ì bá ta èèyàn.

Had Olorun made the black ant as large as a fly, it would have stung us to death.

By the grace of God, the wicked lack the power to do much harm as could otherwise be possible. Bad qualities are needed to balance out the good. But if not for Olorun, bad people would have no good in them at all, and this balance would not exist.

Chapter 3: Who Are the Orishas and Irunmọlẹ?

In the previous chapter, you learned that the Orishas represent the Supreme God, who created Orishas to help and supervise humankind and other living beings. In this one, you'll learn just how fundamental a part the Orishas play as mediators between the human and spiritual realms and why they represent our most influential source of communication with Olofi – and by extension – Olodumare. Learning about the vast number of Orishas you can turn to will enrich your practice and empower you spiritually, mentally, and physically.

Orishas and Irunmole

However, when discussing the role of Orishas in the Yoruba pantheon, there is another term you must familiarize yourself with – and that is Irunmole. While Orishas are a well-known concept for those who are only somewhat familiar with the Yoruba religion, this is certainly not the case with Irunmole. And those who have heard about the latter often confuse them with Orishas themselves. In fact, there is a vast difference between the two concepts. However, despite the well-documented hierarchy among the different beings of the Yoruba pantheon, parts of the traditional legends about the Irunmole are still missing.

What we know is that the term Irunmole is made up of three words: irun (heavenly being), mo (knowledge), and ile (ground). Therefore, the Irunmole are celestial beings in possession of great wisdom who visit the earth. The word can also be a force of nature, even more powerful than energy. This suggests that they are beings made of light rather than energy. Why is this important? It implies that while most Orishas were human beings who have achieved oneness with Olodumare, Irunmole is the force that gives the Orishas the power to achieve that level. Only those who stand for their actions will become known as Orishas, and this is exactly how Obatala, Oshun, and the other famous figures came to be as well. Irunmole helped them establish the evolution of their energy and spirit into the state of Olodumare. And just as there are many different Orishas, there are many Irunmole, who often work together when helping humans. For example, to overcome a difficult hurdle in life, you'll need assistance from Ogun, and the Irunmole Ogun, too.

According to some Yoruba sources, the first 200 Orishas created by Olodumare already possessed Irunmole. In fact, it's possible that these Orishas suggested the creation, including those inhabiting the earth. Initially, they were the only intermediaries between Olofi and mankind, but it is easy to understand their use of their powerful energy to help other creatures. They were also able to take on many forms, much more than some of the lesser Orishas. They formed the celestial community in the skies and regularly called on the Supreme Being, consulting it about their daily duties. As legend has it, they visited so often that Olorun decided to give them a special task to have more peace around the baobab tree. So, when they asked about expanding the universe towards the waters below, Olorun was more than happy to send them to Ife to supervise the evolution of the new life.

Nowadays, an Irunmole is said to be the only presence of the Supreme God on earth. Despite this, it's still capable of maintaining several spiritual and physical forms, including humans and even inanimate objects. According to many contemporary Yoruba practitioners, Irunmole may also empower incorporeal entities if their help is needed during a spell or ceremony. Some of them also consider Olofi as the first Irunmole, which explains why he is the only manifestation of God who communicates with other species. However, all of them agree that, unlike Orishas, Irunmole were never human beings but natural spirits. This is why they can become manifestations of divine power, natural or spiritual energy, or any driving force humans need but find incomprehensible. Only by moving away from their abstract description can one truly understand their importance in human lives. Whether you think of them as spirits of energy and light or highly achieving Orishas with special abilities, they can help you develop and transform your energy, raising it to a much higher plane. Overall, 401 Irunmole are wandering the earth looking for humans to help. If you decide to seek assistance from them, don't forget that you may need the help of a lesser Orisha to facilitate communication with them.

Whereas the Irunmole are seen as light entities, the Orisha are nowadays thought of as almost like humans. Each of them is associated with an aspect of nature in which they express their divine qualities. They can accomplish exemplary feats – which are duly recognized – yet humans can communicate with them. Of course, one must know how to honor an Orisha. Otherwise, they won't work with you. You must learn what they like and don't like to avoid getting on their bad side. While they often work as the intermediaries between man and Olofi or the rest of the divine world, the Orishas can sometimes work against humans as well. Much like humans, they have their likes and dislikes, and if something angers them, they can do just as much harm as they do good.

While this changeable mood can seem like an off-putting quality, this human attitude makes them so relatable. We can see they have their own flaws and virtues, just as we do, and new practitioners are always advised to look for an Orisha they can relate to best. Working with an Orisha allows you to form a personal connection with them. You gain a guide and a counselor in a being you can identify with, and the more you get to know them, the stronger your bond will become. It's also a quality that contributes to the continuity of this belief system, not forgetting its influence on the development of so many contemporary African and South American religions. Fortunately, there are many Orishas a Yoruba practitioner can turn to, and this book will discuss the most important and helpful ones in the following chapters.

Each Orisha has its own prayer bead or eleke and numbers in Yoruba culture. And, despite there being so many, they even recognize each other from their number. Some of them are said to have been present as Irunmole when the earth was created from the ancient water kingdom, while others have come into being much later. These were most likely human beings themselves, who transcended into a semi-divine existence. Each Orisha communicates and manifests differently. Some appear as natural landmarks, such as mountains, rivers, or trees, while others emerge as familiar human beings or animals. According to the ancient Yoruba legends, Orisha didn't know hunger, thirst, and desire at one time as these are all unfamiliar to celestial beings. However, as their numbers grew and they spent more and more time with mankind, they gained the ability to eat, drink, and love – just as humans do. They have also learned to enjoy music, making them easy to appease.

Moreover, each of them has their own favorite foods and other items they like to receive as offerings and gifts. Suppose you make an offering to an Orisha in a way they are accustomed to, and you offer them something they like. In that case, they will recognize the gesture and come to your aid right away. The research will teach you more about their likes and dislikes, and observing the forces of nature they govern is even more helpful. When you conduct your research, remember that Orishas often work together, so you should always observe how the forces of nature interact with each other. For example, the Orisha ruling over rivers will work with the one governing the seas that the rivers flow into. The way the river flows and its rising and falling also reflect Orisha's changeable mood. As you observe their work, you'll get a better understanding of the complex ways of the Orishas. You'll see their celestial force, as well as their human qualities. This will empower you with the knowledge that they are in a way no different from you, making it that much easier to form a deep bond with them. If you manage to establish a mutually respectful relationship with an Orisha, one day, when you need them the most, you may come face to face with them.

Orishas and Ashe

Although their role as messenger between the Supreme God and us cannot be denied, the Orishas can be even more helpful in healing practices. The Orisha's Ashe can subdue misfortune and evil, cleansing your soul and helping it grow until you reach the desired level. For many, this means achieving oneness with Olodumare, but even if your goal is to heal past wounds – Ashe will be of great assistance.

But what is Ashe, and how does it affect you? Ashe is a divine power, the driving force behind everything in the world. Initially, Olodumare gave this energy only to Orisha's living and serving God in the skies. Even when they came up with the idea of creating Ife and humankind, the man wasn't gifted with Ashe as it wasn't deemed necessary for them to have it. Over time, the Supreme God and the Orishas realized that every living being could benefit from this force. For this reason, the Supreme God begins to empower everything with Ashe, including inanimate objects, making it one of the most fundamental concepts in the human belief system. Now, we know it as the immense power behind everything, including our own thoughts, emotions, and actions.

However, Ashe comes to us through only one source – the Orishas. They are the custodians of this flow and can channel it towards us, so it carries us on our journeys. By working with Orishas, you can draw on their Ashe through prayers, offerings, and other ceremonies – ensuring that you stay on the right path. In addition, there are other ways to channel Ashe towards you, particularly for divination or healing. Herbs, colors, candles, and crystals can also initiate its flow towards you, conducting it into you and uniting it with your own energy.

Working with Ashe might be easier than you think, as it is accustomed to receiving voiced words such as prayers, songs, curses, and praises. Sometimes, even an everyday conversation can attract it, encouraging you to make things happen and achieve the change you wish for in your life. For the same reason, you must be very careful how to use it; your entire existence may depend on it! Not only does Ashe have sacred characteristics, but its social ramification often goes beyond anything imaginable. Anyone who learns how to experience and use this essential life force becomes an authority figure. At the same time, through their own initiation, they become subject to its wilful effect that changes their lives forever. You may learn to command this power, but you'll depend on it even more. Except, now you'll know how to employ it in your rituals when invoking particular Orishas or even Olofi should you need their help. Working with an Orisha means recognizing the uniqueness of their Ashe and knowing when they may be useful for you. Recognition of their autonomy is also a sign of respect, which in turn, will earn you their trust and a much more amicable relationship with them.

How Do the Orishas Heal?

When an Orisha comes in contact with your body, it transfers its Ashe to you. However, apart from lending you their Ashe to make you stronger and overcome difficult hurdles in life, Orisha can assist you in many other ways. Each Orisha represents a particular force in the Yoruba pantheon. They all have their own specialties, but they also have specific influences. They can protect and heal nature, and they can do the same for you – you just have to know which one to call upon. According to the powers of the one you choose to work with, an Orisha will protect and defend you, or it may cause disease to go away from the affected part of your body. From physical ailments to emotional scars – we all need healing in many different ways. And while the bond you form with an Orisha will mainly be manifested in your body, this doesn't mean it won't empower your mental state. You exist through your body, so this is the only way the Orishas can connect with you. But once the connection has been made, they will envelop your mind and body, healing you spiritually, if necessary. As mentioned before, you'll most likely need some intermediaries to transfer the energy. Using elements associated with the Orishas will encourage their interaction with your body, ultimately restoring its health and vitality.

What Is an Ebo?

In terms of Yoruba terminology, ebo means sacrifice. However, an ebo can mean a lot of different things as well. It can be offered during different ceremonies and may represent several types of sacrifices. It can be performed as a sacrifice, offering, purification, or an expression of gratitude. Furthermore, the ebo made at each event will depend on the Orishas you are calling on and their likes and dislikes. After a traditional Yoruba ebo, the power of every prayer, spell, or ritual is elevated, and the practitioner's mindset will be focused on manifesting a positive outcome.

There are many types of ebos, and they can be identified by the elements used in them, the offering, and the process used to make the offering. While animal sacrifices were a common occurrence in the past, they aren't required nowadays. The Orisha you call on will be satisfied with a simple offering of fruit and sweets, accompanied by a prayer or perhaps a bath and a display of flowers. Remember, during an ebo, you are cleansing your body from negative energy so that the Orisha's ashe can flow through it more freely. It is considered a medicine that can heal past wounds and solve problems. This is only possible if the sacrifice you make serves your tranquility and health, both physically and mentally. Even if you only do it as a way to please an Orisha in hopes of further collaboration, it will only work if you are keeping a balance in nature as well. After all, the Orishas watch over other beings, not just humans.

Ebo is a common ritual performed prior to the Ifa divination. In this case, it's a combination of rituals that symbolically prepares the person needing the divination. But an ebo is often essential in other types of situations when you want to change your circumstances. Apart from cleansing, an ebo can help identify issues within your spiritual makeup. Having found them, you'll be able to heal them and feel better. Whether you wish to reveal your future or someone else's, need guidance in achieving goals, or seek spiritual enlightenment via the traditional Yoruba ways, you must perform an ebo beforehand. Even if the person for whom the ceremony is performed is in tune with their destiny, performing an ebo will maintain the natural balance of energies.

The ebo sacrifice (or eje) is a specific type of ebo and represents offering the highest power within a living being. While some interpret this as using the blood of an animal, this is far from the truth. In fact, the power and the Orishas ashe flows through the entire animal, and it's the strongest when the animal is alive. This is why many practitioners use living animals during their rituals. For example, you may choose to adopt an animal and nourish its life force, promoting the flow of ashe through it even more. Or you can give it to the person for whom you are performing a ritual so they can take care of it. Another type of animal sacrifice is releasing the creature into nature after the ceremony is concluded. Or the release itself may be fundamental for the ritual's success. This is a common practice in group cleansing rituals before a major festival. Another ebo in which entire communities partake in the celebratory feast. The animals aren't sacrificed in vain but cooked and used as sustenance. It is an act of gratitude towards the Orishas, nature, and the animal that gave its life to feed the people. This is an act that brings harmony and balance into the community and into the life of its individual members.

Chapter 4: Main Female Orishas

We have talked in the previous chapter about Orishas and their role in the Yoruba religion. Up to this day, the Yoruba gods still fascinate people. As the intercessors between the Supreme Deity and humans, the Orishas play a huge role in the Yoruba religion. There are different types of Orishas, and they represent the forces of nature. As mentioned in previous chapters, there are male and female Orishas. In this chapter, we will focus on the main female Orishas.

Ayao

Ayao is the goddess of the air. She lives in the forest or in the sky, and when she travels, she becomes a cyclone or whirlwind. Ayao never touches the ground; for this reason, all her ceremonies take place on a table. She is given to Oya's children, but nowadays, she is given to priests and priestesses. When Oya initiates perform a blessed birth, Ayao tends to the spirits they collect. She uses these spirits to help her sister Oya in battles.

- **Origin Story**

Ayao is the younger sister of Oya, who is another Orisha. She and her sister are highly revered. Ayao lives in the sky to protect the spirits who go through her clouds to live in the Olofi kingdom. She works with the nature Orisha, Osain, from whom she learned magic and botanical knowledge. She uses nine stones, a crossbow, and a quill.

- **Personality**

Ayao is a very powerful and fierce warrior. She is known as a very smart Orisha, and she has an abundance of magic knowledge and witchcraft.

- **Colors**

You'll find the colors associated with Ayao are the colors of leaves and barks – different shades of brown and green.

Oya

Oya is the goddess of the weather. She represents storms, hurricanes, and wind. She is a tall and beautiful woman. She is one of the seven African Powers; she is one of the most powerful and feared Orishas. Women call on this Orisha to help them resolve disputes, which is why she is considered a protector of women. She guards the underworld to help transition the newly dead from our world to the spirit realm. She is also associated with funerals. By rotating her skirt while dancing, Oya can summon tornadoes and lightning. She can alter the cosmos, which is required to bring balance to the universe. Oya can manifest as a beautiful woman or a horned water buffalo. Mothers who suffer from miscarriages and want to get pregnant offer drinks and food to Oya. She cures lung diseases and protects against tornadoes, storms, hurricanes, and lighting.

She can also protect the living from being haunted by the dead.

• **Origin Story**

According to a Yoruba legend, one day, Ogun, the god of war and iron, saw a striking horned water buffalo coming out from the Niger River and transforming into a very beautiful woman. He followed her as she walked like a royal – and couldn't help but fall in love with her. He begged Oya to marry him, but she was hesitant. However, Ogun told her that he knew about her bovine identity and threatened to reveal it if she didn't agree to marry him. They got married, and he loved her passionately. However, during an argument, Ogun accidentally revealed her secret. Oya then left him and married his brother Shango, the god of thunder and lighting. She was his trusted advisor and would fight side by side in battle. However, Oya was barren, so she sacrificed a piece of cloth with the colors of the rainbow. It worked, and she gave birth to 9 children.

• **Personality**

Oya is extremely intellectual and powerful. She is a brave warrior who never backs down from a battle. According to legend, she would grow a beard and wear pants to fight like a man during wars. She is a strong protector, especially to her children, and has helped out every Orisha. This powerful Orisha can summon any natural disaster to destroy men, lands, and cities when angered. She also has psychic abilities that enable her to see things beyond our world.

• Colors

The colors associated with Oya are black, reds, oranges, maroon, and shades of purple.

• Food and Offerings

Oya prefers fruits like purple grapes, purple plums, back grapes, and starfruit. However, her favorite food is eggplants, so a traditional offering for Oya should be nine eggplants. Simply cut one eggplant into nine pieces if you can't afford nine, and nine is the number associated with her since she has nine children. Other offerings for Oya include flowers, red wine, bean fritters, legumes, and tobacco. You can present the offerings by bringing them to cemetery gates or setting up an altar at your home. The best meal for an Oya ritual is nine bean soup or eggplant with rice.

Yewa

Yewa is Oya's sister, and like her sibling, she is also associated with graveyards. She is the goddess of death and virginity. She works with Oya and lives in the cemetery. Yewa is considered the queen of corpses, as she protects them from the moment they die until they are buried. She then delivers them to Oya. According to legend, Yewa would dance over the graves to reassure the dead and let them know they were protected. She also protects the innocent and punishes anyone who disrespects the cult of the dead. It is also believed that Yewa would transform into an owl to perform her guarding duties unnoticed. Since she is also the goddess of virginity, her devotees must remain celibate.

- Origin Story

Yewa wasn't always the goddess of death; she used to be a water Orisha. She is the daughter of Obatala, the sky father and the god of purity, and was known for her exquisite beauty. According to legend, Shango, famous for being a womanizer, seduced Yewa when she was very young and got pregnant. However, she was given a potion that caused her to abort the child. She was devastated by the incident and punished herself by residing in the cemetery. However, there is another version of the myth; it said that she loved Shango but didn't give in to her feelings and remained a virgin. She was ashamed of her feelings and confessed to her father, and he sent her to the realm of the dead, where she remained a celibate.

- Personality

Yewa is mysterious, shadowy, and very regal. She has a very serious personality, and she despises humor, promiscuity, and sexual banter. She also hates cursing, vulgarity, foul language, sexual innuendoes, and any sex discussions, which makes sense since she is the goddess of virginity. Yewa is considered one of the most reclusive Orishas, and she is very diligent, intelligent, wise, knowledgeable, and hardworking.

- Colors

The two colors usually associated with Yewa are scarlet and pink.

- Food and Offerings

As the goddess of death and the queen of cadavers, Yewa would appreciate scented flowers to cover up the odor of dead bodies. You should opt for a large bouquet of flowers to increase the fragrance.

Oba

Oba is the goddess of rivers, and water is her symbol. She represents energy, flexibility, protection, and restoration. In some places, she is considered the goddess of love, while in others, she is the protector of prostitutes. She punishes anyone who takes advantage of a loving heart, just as she was misled while loving her husband – who could not stay true to one woman.

- **Origin Story**

The story of how Oba became the goddess of the River is a very sad one. She was Shango's first wife, but she was aware of her husband's wandering eyes. She didn't mind sharing him as long as she remained his only queen. However, Shango fell madly in love with Oshun and Oya, and he treated them like queens. Oba was extremely frustrated and jealous of how her husband loved these women. According to legend, one of the women tricked Oba and told her that she cut off a piece of her ear, cooked it, and served it to Shango, making him desire her. Oba decided to follow in her rival's footsteps and cut off her ear to serve it to her husband. However, when Shango saw the ear on his food, he was disgusted. Some legends say he left her and never returned, while others say that he thought she wanted to poison him and kicked her out of the house. She then kept crying until her tears created the Oba river. It isn't known exactly *which of the women* tricked Oba, but Oshun was famous for her cooking skills.

- **Personality**

Judging by her sad story, you may think Oba is stupid or weak. However, Oba is a very intelligent woman who is also independent and plays a huge role in politics and commerce. She is also powerful, beautiful, and wealthy. She was just outsmarted by a cunning woman who took advantage of her love for her husband.

- Colors

The colors associated with Oba are red, white, and pink.

- **Food and Offerings**

Oba Orisha prefers flowers, wine, candles, and pond or lake water. Avoid rainwater and spring water. If you plan to cook a meal for this Orisha, opt for beans with shrimp and onions.

Yemoja

Yemoja, who also goes by the name Yemaya is the goddess of the ocean's surface. She represents motherhood and all issues concerning women. She is one of the Seven African Powers. The name Yemaya means " the mother whose children are fish." This name signifies the many devotees she has, which are as numerous as the fish of the sea. Additionally, she has many children since she is the mother of almost all the Orishas. She lives in the sea and is associated with saltwater.

- **Origin Story**

Yemoja is Oshun's sister. She used to live in the graveyard while Oya lived in the sea. Yemoja tricked Oya into trading places with her. Oya never forgave her, which is why these two Orishas should never be revered together.

- **Personality**

Yemoja has many devotees as a result of her kindness and generosity. Her personality resembles that of the sea; she is giving, beautiful, profound, and filled with treasures. However, just like the sea, you should avoid making her angry. She also likes to keep everything and everyone she loves close by.

• Colors

The colors associated with Yemaya are white, pearl, and blue.

• Food and Offerings

To appease Yemaya, opt for perfume, seashells, coral, jewelry, flowers (her favorite are white roses), and scented soap. When it comes to food, this sea goddess prefers watermelon, pomegranate, and all other wet seedy fruits and vegetables. She also enjoys proteins like duck, fish, and lamb. Yemaya prefers coconut cake, pork cracklings, banana chips, and plantain for snacks. You can place the offerings in the ocean or build an altar at your home.

Osun

Osun, also spelled Oshun, is the goddess of the river. She is one of the female deities of the Seven African Powers. She represents love, romance, beauty, and wealth. She dominates anything that flows like honey, water, milk, and even money. Osun has healing abilities for the reproductive organs, among other human body parts. She is usually called on to help with fertility issues and to provide employment, protection, wealth, and love. Oshun usually manifests as a gorgeous woman or a mermaid. She always carries a mirror with her to admire her own beauty.

• Origin Story

According to Yoruba legends, Oldumare, the supreme god, sent male gods with Oshun to create a world on earth. However, the male gods were dismissive of her and her help. Oshun grew tired of not being appreciated and decided to leave. She resided on the moon, where she could be by herself to admire her beauty. She expected the male deity to ask for her help soon. She wasn't wrong, though; everything on earth started to wither, including animals and plants. Oldumare informed them that Earth needed Oshun's love and beauty to survive. The gods begged her to come back, and she did, and the Earth thrived again. It is believed that she is either Yemaya's sister or daughter; for this reason, they are usually venerated together. This isn't the case for Oshun and Oya, though, since both women were married to Shango.

• Personality

Oshun isn't only extremely beautiful, but she is also a powerful warrior. Although she is the sweetest and smallest, Orisha is very tough. She helped Ogun get out of his depression, and she is the only Orisha able to fly to heaven to speak with the Supreme God. Oshun is very generous and incredibly forgiving, which is why she was able to quickly forgive the male deities. She rarely gets angry, but she can be extremely dangerous and hard to appease when she does.

• Colors

Oshun is associated with the colors orange, yellow, and gold.

• Food and Offerings

For the beautiful Oshun, focus on feminine items like brushes, mirrors, perfumes, or makeup. This deity of love would also appreciate flowers. You can also offer her fans made from yellow sandalwood or peacock feathers. When it comes to food and drinks, Oshun loves chamomile tea, and her favorite meal is spinach with shrimp. You should opt for honey if you want to please her since it is her favorite offering. However, you must taste it first, or else the offering will be rejected. This is because someone once tried to poison Oshun with poisoned honey. She also loves orange and yellow vegetables and fruits.

Olokun

Olokun is the deity of the sea. They provide healing, wealth, and fertility. This Orisha's gender, identity, and function vary according to different myths. According to Nigerian legends, Olokun is the king of the sea. He is very powerful and rich, but he didn't survive the Middle Passage slave trade.

• Origin Story

According to another legend, Olokun is female and is either Yemaya's mother, alter ego, or sister. As mentioned, Yemaya is the Orisha of the surface of the sea or ocean, and Olokun is the goddess of the deepest and darkest parts of the sea. She is the Orisha of life and death. It is believed life emerged from the sea, and the realm of death is at the bottom of the sea. Olokun controls the area souls have to cross to either be born or return to death's realm. Olokun can heal pain and any kind of abuse, whether physical or mental. Her abilities extend to healing pain and abuse that occurred before birth or speech.

- **Personality**

Olokun prefers to be alone, and she is usually silent and brooding.

- **Colors**

The colors associated with Olokun are beige and blue.

- **Food and Offerings**

This Orisha prefers offerings related to the sea like saltwater and seashells.

Nana Buruku

Nana Buruku is the supreme goddess, the creator, and the great grandmother of all the Yoruba deities. She is the most respected and admired Orisha, and she represents swamps, mud, clay, and marshes. She is usually called on to help provide medicinal herbs that can heal various ailments. She can also identify and cure diseases that doctors can't understand or treat. Additionally, Nana Buruku is called on by people who suffer from infertility. She also guards the dead and manifests as a very old woman.

- **Origin Story**

According to legend, this supreme goddess gave birth to the sun (Lisa) and the moon (Mawu). Afterward, she retired and entrusted the world to her children. It is believed that Nana Buruku used magic to create humans and the cosmos, and her twin children were the first man and woman.

- **Personality**

Nana Buruku is a very brave warrior and a fierce witch. Her generosity knows no bounds when it comes to the people she loves. However, you should never anger her, or she will infect you with diseases.

- **Colors**

The colors associated with this supreme deity are white, black, pink, and dark blue.

- **Food and Offerings**

To appease Nana Buruku, focus on plant-based offerings like roses, swamp plants, mandrakes, or any other roots.

Abata

Abata is the Orisha of marshes and swamps. She has the power to make someone either wealthy or poor. She usually controls places where saltwater and freshwater merge, like in swamps. She can provide emotional balance, health, and peace.

- ## Origin Story

According to Yoruba legends, Abata is the wife of Erinle, the Orisha of wealth. However, other legends believe she is his counterpart, and they can merge together. Unlike her husband, there isn't much known about her. This is probably because she is a swamp, Orisha, and swamps are usually associated with hidden treasure and secrets.

- ## Personality

Abata is very powerful and hardworking. She is famous for her vast knowledge as well.

- ## Colors

The colors associated with Abata are the shades of her necklace beads: green, blue, and yellow. Other colors associated with her are gold, coral, and pink.

- ## Food and Offerings

Abata's favorite food includes roasted yam, sweet potatoes, and snapper. She also enjoys panetela, almond oil, sweet guava, and almond balls. She will be very pleased if you offer her white wine since it is her favorite drink. She also likes fruits and flower arrangements, melons, and grapes. Abata prefers her offerings to be brought to her home in the swamps.

Aja

Aja is considered one of the most popular Orishas. She is the goddess of forests and animals. She is also a healer who uses the medicinal plants in her forests to heal the sick. Aja loves sharing her knowledge which is why people like shamans call on her to bestow her knowledge on them. Aja isn't like other Orishas because she will reveal herself to humans with no intention of scaring or harming them but teaching them how to make healing herbs.

• Origin Story

Aja lives in the forest, where she makes potions to help the sick. According to legends, she is the wife of the sea god Oloku and Yemaya's mother.

• Personality

Aja is a healer and a strong warrior who shouldn't be provoked.

• Colors

Since she is the Orisha of the forest, Aja is associated with the color green.

Chapter 5: Main Male Orishas

The Yoruba religion, which originated in West Africa, is home to a plethora of deities and supernatural creatures, including supreme beings and the Orishas, the intermediaries between mankind and the divine. Previously, we learned of the female Orishas; this chapter covers their male counterparts. Male Orishas are best understood through examining the natural forces with which they are associated.

Aganjú

In Yoruba mythology, Aganju is associated with volcanoes, the wilderness, and rivers. Thought to be one of the oldest of the Orishas, Aganju is rumored to be the third deity who came to earth. Aganju is considered a cultivator of growth and civilization, both of which are linked to his symbol, the sun. Like a volcano, Aganju can bring about a drastic change in society and is the foundation upon which societies are built.

- **Origin Story**

  Aganju was supposedly a king in the Oyo Empire in Yoruba history. He was the fourth Alaafin of Oyo (which means "owner of the palace" or king in Yoruba) and was greatly loved by his people. Before he ascended the throne, he was a warrior and used to carry a double-edged sword everywhere with him.

- **Personality**

  He loved nature and used to explore the wilderness for days. One time, he came back with a leopard and domesticated it. Even while living among humans, Aganju was no ordinary man. He was rumored to have spiritual and unimaginable powers and an ability to domesticate wild animals.

- **Colors**

  The colors (or, more accurately, the *bead pattern*) associated with Aganju are two brown, one red, one yellow, one blue, one yellow, one red, and two brown.

- **Food and Offerings**

  Aganju likes offerings of alcoholic drinks and beef food items.

Babalù Ayé

Associated with disease and healing, Babalù Ayé is considered the spirit of the earth. Consequently, he controls everything earthly, including health, wealth, and any physical assets. His name roughly translates as "Father, Lord of the earth." In earlier Yoruba beliefs, he was mainly linked to smallpox, and other epidemics, whereas modern Yoruba beliefs associate him with AIDS, influenza, and other infectious diseases. Although most people associate Babalù Ayé with the disease, he is also the patron of healing and is both feared and loved.

- **Origin Story**

  From the ancient Yoruba mythology folklore, Babalù Ayé's origin story is commonly retold by many Yoruba followers. Once, Shopona (common name for Babalù Ayé in Yoruba tradition) attended a party at the Orisha's, where he stumbled and fell. When the other Orishas laughed at him, he tried to inflict smallpox on them but was stopped and exiled by his father.

- **Personality**

  Although many beliefs in Yoruba depict Babalù Ayé as someone to fear, he is also a merciful and humble Orisha. He is associated with healing as much as with disease. He also helps people with terminal diseases to get peace by guiding their souls to the other side.

- **Colors**

  The sacred colors associated with Babalù Ayé are blue, yellow, and purple.

- **Food and Offerings**

  The food offerings Babalù Ayé favors are black-eyed peas, beans, popcorn, rum, and tobacco.

Erinlẹ̀

Erinlẹ̀, commonly known as the elephant of the earth in Yoruba, is considered the deity associated with healing, medicine, and comfort. One of the most fiercely celebrated Orishas, Erinlẹ̀, is the underwater king, as well as the spirit of the bush. Erinlẹ̀ has two sides, as a water spirit and healer – and a hunter of the forest and a warrior.

- **Origin Story**

  According to Yoruba tradition, Erinlẹ̀ was a hunter before he became an Orisha. He is said to have protected the town of Fulani from attackers. He used to live in the forest, in a hut he had made for himself. Some myths claim that one day he sank into the earth near Ilobu, where he first conducted Olobu and became a river.

- **Personality**

  Envisioned as one of the wealthy deities, he is dressed in luxurious and beautiful clothes, combined with accessories from the sea and forest. As a deity associated with earth, he is masculine and mighty.

- **Colors**

  Being associated with rivers and the forest, the colors of patron Erinlẹ̀ are turquoise, coral, and green.

Èṣù

Èṣù, pronounced Eshu, is considered the trickster Orisha in Yoruba tradition. He is full of tricks and pranks that can often be cruel and are sometimes harmful. Known to speak all the languages on earth, the messenger deity, Èṣù, conveys messages from the gods to people. He's also said to carry the offerings people send to different Orishas.

- **Origin Story**

  Yoruba mythology tells of how Èṣù became the messenger. Due to his love for pranks and tricks, he played one on the high god, in which he stole his ham, used his slippers to make footprints, and tried to convince the high god that he stole the ham himself. The god got annoyed and told Èṣù to visit the land every day and tell him about the occurrences at night.

- **Personality**

  Èṣù is an embodiment of mischief and loves to cause trouble. He likes to be appeased to fulfill his duties of conveying messages to and fro. This deity often makes use of trickery to teach lessons.

- **Colors**

  The colors used to identify the Orisha god of mischief are red and black or white and black.

Ibeji

Ibeji are a set of twin Orishas sacred to the Yoruba tradition. The word Ibeji roughly translates to two-born. Twins are thus considered to be sacred to the people of Yoruba. They have the highest rate of twin births as compared to the rest of the world. The Ibeji are considered one Orisha and are said to have one soul in two bodies. They are associated with joy, mischief, and glee.

- ## Origin Story

  Oshun, the mother of Ibeji, was shunned by people when she gave birth to twins because twin births were supposedly unusual at that time. Only animals could give birth to multiple, identical offspring. So, the people labeled Oshun a witch and shunned her. Because of this, Oshun refused to accept Ibeji as her own offspring and threw them out of her house. Oya later adopted the Ibejis.

- ## Personality

  Considered to be the protector of children, Ibeji Orisha is always represented as a baby or small child. Although depicted as this, Ibeji is a warrior in Yoruba history.

- ## Colors

  Usually, red, white, and sometimes blue colors are associated with Ibeji.

- ## Food and Offerings

  Food offerings for Ibeji are usually beans, sugarcane, pumpkin, ekuru, vegetables, red-palm oil, and cake.

Ọbàtálá

Ọbàtálá is known for creating the human body and the sky and is therefore also called the sky father. Rumored to be the oldest Orisha, Ọbàtálá comes among one of the white Gods of creativity. The word Ọbàtálá is broken and translated to Oba, which means king, and tala, which means undyed fabric. More commonly, Ọbàtálá is considered to be the father of all Orishas and mankind. Ọbàtálá is associated with wisdom, purity, peacefulness, and compassion.

- ## Origin Story

  Ọbàtálá came down to earth from heaven to mold the bodies of the first humans. In addition to the primordial Ọbàtálá, his mortal counterpart was the founder and king of Ile-Ife. The Orisha Ọbàtálá hence originated as a mixture of the two.

- **Personality**

  Ọbàtálá is described as a gentle and peace-loving Orisha associated with forgiveness, resurrection, honesty, and purpose. Also commonly known as the king of the white cloth, Ọbàtálá is said to be an extremely tranquil judge.

- **Colors**

  The color associated with Ọbàtálá is pure white, representing the purity he brings.

- **Food and Offerings**

  Food offerings made to Ọbàtálá are white in color to represent purity. These include rice, meringue, cocoa butter, and coconut.

Odùduwà

Odùduwà is considered one of the reigning ancestors among the kings of Yoruba. More commonly known as the Orisha of humans. His name roughly translates into the hero, the warrior, the father, and the leader of the Yoruba race. According to Yoruba tradition, Odùduwà was Olodumare's favorite Orisha, and he held an important role in the story of creation.

- **Origin Story**

  Odùduwà was one of the deities involved in the task of developing the earth's crust. After Obatala got drunk on palm wine and was unable to develop the land, Odùduwà was sent to complete his task. The point on earth where he jumped from heaven and converted into land was named Ile-Ife, which is now considered the heart of Yorubaland.

- **Personality**

  Odùduwà was a conquering warrior associated with creation, salvation, and power. He had no recognizable human form and is said to dwell deep in the darkness. Sometimes, he is referred to as the king of the dead in Yoruba tradition.

- **Colors**

  Although Odùduwà is associated with death, his colors are white and opal.

Òún

Ogun, also called the Orisha of iron, is known as the father of civilization in Yoruba mythology. He is said to be a protector of his people and a very just leader. Known for his creativity and intelligence, he invented the many tools humans needed for their survival. Otherwise, the earth would have remained a wilderness. He is also known for his strength and sacrifice. He supposedly cleared the path for his fellow Orisha to come to earth with his knives.

- **Origin Story**

  Ogun's origin story tells how he ended up being the Orisha of iron. The Orisha and humans are said to have once existed together on land. Both of them leveled land to create more space to live. However, when the population increased, it became more and more difficult to find land and cultivate it. The tools used at that stage were made of wood, stone, or soft metal. One by one, all the Orisha tried to clear the land. However, none of them were able to succeed. This was when Ogun cleared the path with his iron knives. The other Orisha then made him a ruler in exchange for his knowledge about iron but later banned him. However, humans still remember and worship him to this day.

- **Personality**

  There are two sides to the personality of Ogun; protective, fierce, and bloodthirsty versus creative, innovative, and intelligent. He can be the angriest warrior out of all Orisha at times while also showing a creative and calm side when designing his tools. He liked to hunt with his hand-crafted tools in densely forested areas.

- **Colors**

  Being the Orisha of iron and war, the colors associated with Ogun are green, red, and black signifying the forest, fire, and war.

- **Food and Offerings**

  Ogun prefers sacrificial offerings of catfish, alligator pepper, palm wine, roosters, red palm oil, and the like.

Okó

Oko is considered the farming and fertility deity among the Orishas. He is said to hold the secrets to farming and maintaining fertility in crops. He maintains the stability of life through his rotation of crops which provides humans with nutrition to survive. Oko is also the judge of Orishas and jumps to the defense of any female when an argument arises.

- **Origin Story**

  Oko was given a piece of mechanical contraption by Ogun to help with his crops. It consisted of two oxen, which he became symbolized by. He was the first one to build a farm and cultivate the land to feed his family.

- **Personality**

  Oko has a warm and harmonious personality. He is all about growth and the cultivation of life. Moreover, he is a trusted advisor for women and helps infertile women bear children.

- **Colors**

  Oko is associated with the colors light blue and pink.

- **Food and Offerings**

  Food offerings made to Oko can include all sorts of harvest food, dried meat, beans, yams, and slugs.

Osanyin

Osanyin is largely associated with plants, healing, and magic. He is a strong wizard, well respected for his magical abilities. He is the deity who has extensive knowledge of the medicinal purposes of herbs, roots, leaves, and plants. Many faith rituals in Yoruba involve Osanyin's plants and herbs.

- **Origin Story**

  Osanyin was a crippled Orisha, missing one leg and one arm, and was blind in one eye. However, his brother Orunmila wanted Osanyin to feel better, so he asked Osanyin to pull out weeds from the crops early in the morning. When Orunmila returned the following evening, he found his brother crying in the field, having picked not a single weed out. When asked why Osanyin replied with the various healing abilities of different plants present there, his brother was astonished at the level of knowledge Osanyin had regarding plants. Since then, Osanyin has been declared the deity of plants, herbs, and healing.

- **Personality**

  Osanyin loved nature and liked to collect knowledge about the various plants and herbs he found present in the forest. He has extensive healing abilities and is considered kind and humble.

- **Colors**

  The various colors associated with Osanyin are green, yellow, black, red, and white.

- **Food and Offerings**

  Typical food offerings for Osanyin are meat, nuts, chili, etc.

Oṣùmàrè

The name Oṣùmàrè roughly translates to rainbow, and that is exactly what Oṣùmàrè is associated with. Residing at the back of the mountains, Oṣùmàrè's duty is to fill the sky with beautiful colors to convey messages from the earth to heaven and vice versa. He is associated with unity and peace and symbolizes the balance between humans and Orisha.

- **Origin Story**

  When the earth was created, the Orishas and divinities came into existence. Oṣùmàrè was ordered to signal a rainbow across the sky, indicating the creation of the universe was complete. Oṣùmàrè carries messages from Oluron, ruler of heaven to earth.

- **Personality**

  Oṣùmàrè controls change, movement, and mobility. He is all about transformations and cyclic processes. His personality is very kind and giving. He loves the humans very much and showers them with blessings. He also controls rain and drought. He is also said to be the protector of children and controls the umbilical cord since it is considered the link between our world and that of our ancestors.

- **Colors**

  The colors associated with Oṣùmàrè are white and silver. White is the color through which the different prism of rainbow colors is formed.

- **Food and Offerings**

  Oṣùmàrè's favorite food is boiled white corn with coconut. He also likes rum.

Ṣàngó

Ṣàngó is one of the most powerful rulers in the Yoruba empire. Ṣàngó is also associated with thunder and lightning. Considered one of the most powerful and feared Orisha, he strikes anyone who offends him with lightning.

- **Origin Story**

  In addition to the primordial existence of Ṣàngó, his earthly existence is also worth noting. He was the third Alaafin of Oyo and brought prosperity to the empire. His reign lasted seven years and was ended abruptly because his palace was destroyed by lightning.

- **Personality**

  He was a violent and aggressive ruler, unlike his brother Ajaka. However, this violence came with commendable courage to fight many battles throughout his reign. Thus, he is worshiped with the strong beats of the Bata drum.

- **Colors**

  The colors associated with Ṣàngó are mainly red and white. The bead pattern varies in groups of four and six, which are his sacred numbers.

• Food and Offerings

The sacred food associated with Ṣàngó is amala, a stew of okra mixed with palm oil and shrimp.

Chapter 6: How Ifa Divination Peeks into the Future

Since the beginning of time, divination has been an aspect of all cultural experiences and practice, in one way or another. This practice comes in numerous forms across the globe. It can be diagnostic, in the sense that it's used to detect illnesses or ailments, forecasting, implying that it's used to determine future events, and interventionist, so that practitioners use it to change the destinies of their clients. Some forms of divination that the Ancient Greece prophets practiced involved the belief that the practitioner had experienced direct contact with a supernatural entity. This is often known as inspirational divination. Other forms, however, which were practiced by Mongolian Shamans, Yoruba priests of divination, and African basket diviners, require a type of trained skill.

Divination Techniques

Many believe that you need both skill and inspiration to practice most forms of divination. The elements of nature are what shape divination activities. This explains why they are nature-based and can be carried out using natural materials like water, nuts, bones, and tea leaves. The use of cards and other man-made materials is also very common. There are also spontaneous forms of divination, which can include observing the behavior of birds. African people use many different types of divination, which often don't rely on using objects. For instance, Malian Doon diviners draw box-like shapes on the sandy soil, then arrange food, symbols, and sticks within them. They use words or invocations and call upon a fox to set the process in motion and reveal answers to their clients' questions. When the fox comes to eat, the objects in the box get moved around. The diviner receives his answers by reading the traces left by the animal.

Other African divination techniques rely on objects to get to the other realm. The Democratic Republic of Congo's Kuba uses *itombwa* or friction oracles carved by artists. These oracles are carved in the shape of elephants, crocodiles, wild pigs, and especially dogs. On very rare occasions, a human figure placed horizontally and over a four-legged animal is used. These oracles are used as a means of communication with the spirits of nature to aid in diagnosing the causes and cures of illnesses, the identification of malefactors, and eliminating other problems that may act as a threat to society.

The Popularity of the Yoruba Ifa Divination

The Yoruba Ifa divination, which will be explored in this chapter, is among the most well-known divination techniques. This is perhaps the result of the vast amount of research into the Yoruba, religion, and people. This heightened interest is perhaps due to the strong association between the Yoruba in Africa and the Americas. Plenty of the elements present in the Yoruba belief system have survived the passage of time; some have even been *reinvented.* This is because many of the enslaved people during the slave trades to be sent to the "New World" were Yoruba people brought from West Africa. Being pulled away from their people and home, the Yoruba insisted on keeping their traditions alive. Slave owners and missionaries took extreme measures to ensure that the African culture would be entirely stamped out. However, despite their efforts, the Yoruba always found a way to keep their beliefs alive. For this reason, many religious elements were maintained and still flourish in the Americas today. The preservation of Yoruba concepts, along with the renewed interest in traditional African religions, is exactly why you can find a Yoruba diviner in any of the United States' large cities.

Reading this chapter will help you learn the Ifa divination practice, how it works, and when it is used. We will describe what the 256 Odu are and how the sacred palm nuts and the divination chain are used. Finally, you'll also understand what a *Babalawo* is and how you can become one.

Ifa Divination

The Yoruba have various divination practices. However, they believed Ifa divination to be the most intricate and accurate of all their practices. This form of divination is related to the use of mathematics and a robust structure of oral tales and poems. Ifa is central to the Yoruba's culture, society, and religion. It is thought to incorporate a vital source of cosmology, belief system, and knowledge. The term *Ifa* points to both the Yoruba god of divination, also known as Orunmila, and the divination practice itself. The divination practice is common in many West African groups, especially the Fon people from the Republic of Benin.

One method known as the Ifa method of divination involves performing a full ritual where the diviner, a priest, the client, and the Yoruba people's cosmological and social order have to interact. This is the only way in which helpful answers can be found to the questions asked by clients. The Ifa divination practice occurs when a client asks for help from the order of supernatural beings with undetectable issues. Most clients tend to seek answers related to journeys, the nation's fate, such as a successor to the king, promising marriages, or illnesses. The greatest thing about Ifa is that it is open to everyone, which means that no problems are considered too complex, hard, irrelevant, or small when consulting Ifa. The Yoruba have high confidence and a deep belief in Ifa, which is why it governs the moral order and cosmology of the Yoruba. Ifa has been declared the deity source of knowledge of everything that exists in the universe. The deity is mentioned as an all-knowing storyteller and is the middleman between the people and the other gods and a historian. He is the deity of wisdom and intellect and the Yoruba's public relations handler. Also, Ifa takes on the role of the Yoruba all-powerful healer. For that, the deity is highly respected and valued among the members of society. When a client's ailment is assigned and determined by a diviner, the appropriate sacrifice is conducted, and healing occurs.

How It Works

The Ifa divination process occurs when a diviner is asked for consultation and casts the opele, or the divining chain, on a divining mat. The diviner may use sixteen palm nuts to come to a solution. The results of the divination process are known as the Signs or *Signature of Ifa*. Essentially, the results are usually one of 256 viable signs. The manipulation of the divining chain's 16 palm nuts results in a double tetragram, which is considered the result. The diviner then uses their finger to trace the *Signature of Ifa*. The diviner is also supposed to sprinkle *iyerosun,* a yellow divining powder, over the *Opon Ifa* or divining tray's surface, making the signs clearer. The diviner announces the results, and he chants. This process is also supposed to invoke the Signature of the Ifa deity, who delivers a message that the diviner should recite. The diviner should then clarify the message to their client and assign them the sacrifices they should conduct.

The 256 Odu

As you may recall, the Yoruba religion is founded upon scriptures of oral literature. These scriptures are known as the *Ifa Corpus* or the *Odu Ifa*. The Odu Ifa is a set of Ifa spiritual traditions, historical data, cultural information, and everlasting wisdom. This blend of knowledge has been put together through the centuries by using divination, interactions with the universe, and physical experiences and events. Diviners continue to enrich their knowledge and life journey by referring to this source of infinite wisdom.

Many followers refer to the *Odu Ifa* as the blueprint of life. This source is believed to act as a form of guidance for humanity. It allows humans to move positively toward manifesting their fates and making it through challenging periods in life. An accurate interpretation of the *Odu Ifa* can help answer questions and determine unknown outcomes.

The Yoruba oral tradition suggests that the 16 Odu were originally 16 divine prophets. Those heavenly entities supposedly came to Earth and made themselves known to the prophet of Ifa religion and wisdom, *Orunmila*. According to another oral tradition. Orula and Odudwa had 16 children together, considered symbols of the 16 vital Odu. These Odu Ifa signs are the basis of Ifa tradition and are where the other 240 Ifa signs come from.

The centuries' worth of wisdom and knowledge regarding spiritual enlightenment, moral philosophies, ethics, life experiences, sacrifices, rituals, etc., are represented by the Odu. This information is presented in the form of *ese*, meaning verse. Each Odu integrates information with two sides: the good and the bad. It includes instruction on how to manifest the good and guidance on how to curb and diminish negative, intrusive forces.

The 256 Odu Ifa is the entire set of Ifa Corpus, with the 16 previously mentioned Odu being its pillars. The basis of the Ifa religion is made up of 256 Odu in total. A practitioner must serve an intensive and rigorous apprenticeship to give an accurate reading. This process can take 15 to 30 years, and sometimes even more. This is because the diviners must memorize the entire collection of the Ifa verses.

Becoming a Babalawo

The Yoruba diviners are known as the Babalawo. Anyone who wants to become an Ifa priest, or a *Babalawo*, must be ready to dedicate their existence to Ifa and Olodumare. The term *Babalawo* can be translated into the *"Father of the Mysteries or Secrets of the Earth."* Becoming a Babalawo is the pursuit of a lifetime and is only suitable for individuals who wish to submit themselves to the practice and incorporate it into their lifestyles not only as a career but as a calling and lifestyle.

It is standard procedure to ask an individual who wishes to become an Ifa priest a set of questions designed to validate their motivation to become a priest. Traditionally, those who want to learn about Ifa for meat will receive an abundance of meat, those who wish to do it for money will get a lot of money, and people who wish to practice gaining many wives will get many wives. However, those who wish to become an Ifa priest in pursuit of the truth will gain all the riches in life, including the meat, money, and wives. While these questions may be a little dated, the principle behind them is that those who practice divination to seek the truth are better off than those who do it for personal gain or interest.

There are numerous procedures to be followed on the journey to becoming a *Babalawo*. If not completed under the guidance of a priest or master, the apprentice will never truly be a *Babalawo*. The first step includes the completion of the Ounje Oju Opele, or the food of Opele ritual. This ritual comprises numerous steps that must be completed in order. After eating the food of Opele, the master will open the 16 Odu Ifa with the Akaragba, which is made for the calabash that is used to conduct sacrifices to Esu, the apprentice, for five days. The Akaragba must be used when learning about Ifa and must be kept safe for life. Those who are fast learners may be exposed to the Odu more quickly. After the apprentice learns to open the Oju Odu Merindinlogun, they move on to the next step, divination. This is followed by learning how to receive answers to "yes" and "no" questions. In this step, the student learns about an Odu that helps with divination. Afterward, they learn how to make an ibo, characterized by aspects of good and bad. The master will teach the apprentice the elements of each and the differences between male and female readings. Then, the student will start learning about the Odu Ifa. They must memorize them too. This process may take a very long time, depending on the apprentice's memory.

After a while, the student will progress to learning how to make sacrifices and feed all the Orisha. The apprentice will also start learning about the elements of Ifa and the accompanying Odu Ifa, along with its negative and positive facets. The student must also learn how to create medicines for a wide array of ailments. All this information must be memorized well, as the student can't refer to notes or books for guidance. A person's initiation to Ifa doesn't mean that they've become a Babalawo. It simply means that their learning journey has started.

From the moment we were created, we have always used a wide array of methods in hopes of making sense of the world around us. Think of the I Ching of China, the tarot cards of Europe, and even the spider divination techniques of the Incans. African divination is no different from any of the others. It uses random objects and techniques to forge a connection with the spiritual realm and identify the causes and solutions to problems. Practitioners of divination are mentored by specialists and undergo training to become masters. Clients visit diviners who live elsewhere. This is because local diviners can use information that they heard about the client's work or family situations to connect the dots and give a reading. Meanwhile, visiting a stranger would force the diviner to rely solely on their methods of connecting with the spiritual realm.

Chapter 7: Honoring Your Ancestors

Ancestors play a critical role in the Yoruba religious system. They provide a link between what we can see and the invisible. This chapter discusses the significance of ancestors and the steps you can take to honor them. It also provides instructions on how to create an ancestor altar.

Significance of Ancestors

You can talk to the ancestors and ask for guidance and help when you need it. Since ancestors once lived as humans on earth, they better understand our needs, wants, and desires. However, this is a two-way street – you need to honor the lives of your ancestors if you want to get the help you need. Like any other religion in any other part of the world, ancestors are commemorated for their struggles, triumphs, and work they do for the living people. They drink what we drink, eat what we eat, do what we do, and go wherever we go. Therefore, we need to honor our ancestors to appreciate their presence in our lives.

Building an Ancestor Shrine

In the Yoruba religion, it is believed that everyone has an obligation and can communicate with their ancestors daily. If you want to communicate with your ancestor, you don't need any special knowledge or skills. Communicating with the ancestors is a simple gesture where you remember the departed when you make important decisions in life. The wisdom we get from our parents' folklore or oral tradition is enough to help us talk to the ancestors.

The most common method of communicating with the ancestors is through dreams. Taking part in festivals and other ancestor ceremonies which honor their existence in our lives is how you can get the information you are seeking. When honoring your ancestors, you should have a shrine, and there are different Yoruba methods you can consider building one. You should construct a shrine if you can access the lineage of your elders. Consult the ancestors for guidance when you gather the required things. Modifications and other elements can come later once your shrine is in place.

When you complete your shrine, you can communicate directly with your ancestors through activities like divination, visions, and other states of mental consciousness. You should get a bundle of nine sticks which you should tie with a red cloth. A priest with knowledge of Yoruba rites must identify the tree where you can collect the twigs. This bundle of sticks will be placed on your shrine, and this is where you'll present all your offerings, including food, drink, and animals.

Creating an Altar

As an alternative to a shrine, you can also build an altar where you'll perform your rituals to honor the ancestors. Find an area in your home or outside that you can use for prayer and meditation. You should put appropriate items on the altar and keep it clean. It is believed that dirt attracts evil spells and negative energy. You can use smoke to cleanse your altar. It is common in Yoruba tradition to find weeds with an aromatic scent and place them in a clay pot. Light the weeds to create smoke and make sure it reaches all the rooms if your altar is inside the house.

As you fan the smoke into each room of your house, say a prayer is asking the ancestors to remove negative energy from your home. The container you choose for this particular purpose should be reserved for ritual work only and keep it at your shrine. You can say the following prayer to appease the ancestors to remove negative elements.

"I pay homage to the spirits of the ancestors.

I am (state your name) the child of (mention your lineage).

I pay homage to the spirit of leaves.

Send away the spirit of death.

Send away illness.

Send away all gossip."

You say this prayer directly to the leaves. When you finish your prayer, breathe on the leaves, and say the word used to lock the prayer. The word also indicates that the invocation is over. Keep your thoughts focused on the intention of cleansing. It is crucial to have your altar in a neutral environment so that you'll be able to invite ancestors to your shrine. Emotional energy can linger in a room, which is why you should periodically clean the area to get rid of it.

Cleansing the altar should follow the same procedure you take when cleaning your body. The smoke should be fanned in the same direction. After performing the cleansing ritual, seal it with herbs and water. There are different types of herbs that can be used for locking in positive energy. Clearwater can be mixed with *efun or cascaria. Efun* is a white substance made from fossilized seashells. You can add cologne or other special types of fragrance to the water. Ideally, a scent you wear periodically. Put some fluids obtained from your body, like saliva or urine, into the water. This is an act of adding your presence to the seal. This will be a statement to the spirit realm to mark your invitation to your ancestors to enter.

You can use a traditional *Ifa* prayer to enhance the power of the water. Additionally, you need to say an enhancement prayer so you can include any other things you want. The following prayer will provide an ancestral invitation.

"I pay homage to the spirit of water

I am your child

Bring me

The good fortune of peace

The fortune of a stable home

Good fortune to my children

The good fortune of an abundance

The good fortune of long life

The good fortune of an ancestor shrine

The good fortune of the blessing brought by my higher self from the realm of the ancestors."

Say this prayer to the water. When you finish, sprinkle the water in all the places that the smoke has cleansed. When you are working on the sacred space, you should apply your conscious mind in everything you do. It is vital to welcome the ancestors to the altar as part of honoring them.

You also need to exclude ancestors who displayed violent or addictive behavior. The presence of such ancestors at your shrine can introduce similar influences, which will be a curse on your family. You need to identify the problems you don't want at your shrine. Once you identify the spirits who are welcome, you can start communicating with them directly to honor them. As your skills of communicating with the spirits develop, you can construct your ancestor altar. This should come after the cleansing ceremony.

An altar is a place where we remember the departed people who have joined the spiritual world. It's a place where we consider the wisdom of our lineage and determine how it will inform and guide us through different problems we may encounter. Your construction must be simple, and you should avoid complicated things. When you use a box, make sure you cover it with a white cloth and place a glass of water and a candle on top. These are basic elements that create human beings, representing the earth, fire, air, and water.

You can use the walls behind your altar to display the images of your relatives. By seeing a picture of your revered ancestor, you are reminded of how they solved different issues during their lifetime. Remembering is also a good practice since it inspires and resolves challenging issues we may encounter. Images of the ancestors constantly remind us of their contributions and how they continue to guide us.

We all come from diverse backgrounds and have encountered a variety of spiritual influences. Most people get into contact with these spiritual influences through reading different books like the Bible, Koran, I Ching, or Buddhist Sutra. You should combine these spiritual influences with Ifa to understand different worldviews.

You must light your candle on the altar and stand in front of it to honor your ancestors. The other thing you should do is to show your commitment to the altar you use for your daily prayers and meditation. You must develop self-discipline with regard to the way you use your altar.

For instance, you can commit to using your sacred space at least one day a week. Do not commit yourself to an agreement you cannot honor since this can cause distrust among your ancestors.

When you agree with your ancestors over how you'll communicate with them, you form a spiritual connection with them. Elements like cloth, water sources, candles, and pictures attract the spirit to the shrine. The prayers you say on your altar will cement the connection between you and the ancestors.

You should always turn to your sacred altar regardless of your situation to strengthen the flow of the currents. You should not only remember your altar when you are going through difficult times; *that can weaken the current of your prayer.* It should be charged regularly, so you must dedicate time to remembering your departed relatives daily. You also need to imagine how your role models can help solve different challenges you may encounter.

Ancestor Offering

Another great way of honoring your ancestors is to make food offerings to the altar. In Yoruba, this type of offering is called *adimu egun*. The purpose of making an offering is to create reciprocity where we ask the ancestors for guidance while we give them something in return. The ancestors eat and drink the same things as us, so offering them similar items is a great way of honoring them. Food offerings do not necessarily mean your ancestors are hungry, but it is just a gesture to show that you remember them.

In Yoruba tradition, you must present a small portion of food at the edge of your eating mate as a sign to honor your ancestors. You can also use a plate in front of your Egun altar to provide your food offering. The plate is a symbol of the body that is buried underneath the earth when the spirit rises to the other world. The food offering is traditional, and drinks often accompany it.

Traditional alcoholic beverages are often used in African traditions as part of the honoring exercise. Alternatively, you can also place a cup of coffee or tea on the altar to accompany your food offering in the plate.

You can also use flowers as direct offerings to the ancestors. You place them on the altar, and some people can also use cigars to honor their ancestors. The smoke is used to cleanse the place. Once you establish a communication link with the ancestors, they will tell you the things they want as offerings. Try to follow the instructions provided by the ancestors for guidance. Express gratitude and thank the ancestors when you finish presenting your offering.

You should feed your ancestors regularly to honor them for everything they do for you. This can go a long way in helping keep the ancestors close to your altar. In Africa, most people provide an offering of food before they drink anything. When you live in a foreign country, you must make a weekly offering. If you maintain a schedule, you'll not need to feed your ancestors regularly.

When you are not initiated, your ancestor shrine will provide an alternative system you can use for divination. These divination practices are based on Odu Ifa. The divination is usually directed at a particular spirit, and the spirit will bring messages from different sources. However, invocations meant to open divination are directed at a specific Orisa or Egun.

The ancestors form an integral part of our lives since they are ever-present in whatever we do. They eat and drink the same things, just like human beings. The ancestors provide us wisdom and guidance in different things we may need to achieve. However, to get what we want from our ancestors, we need to honor them to express our gratitude for their good work. We have discussed different methods we can consider honoring our ancestors. You need a shrine to perform any ritual directed to your ancestors, and you must decorate your sacred place with the right items.

More importantly, there are certain prayers you should recite when you present an offering to your ancestors. Close each session with appropriate words to thank them.

Chapter 8: Yoruba Worship Calendar and Holy Days

Just like the Yoruba people have their own language, they have their own calendar and holy days as well. The Yoruba calendar is called KỌ́JỌ́DÁ, which means "may the day be clearly foreseen." Their year begins on June the 3rd of the Gregorian calendar and ends on June the 2nd of the next year. The year 2022 AD is the 10,064th Yoruba year.

The Yoruba calendar has 12 months in its year like the Georgian calendar, but this is where the similarities end. The weeks are longer in the Yoruba calendar as there are 91 weeks, but the days are shorter with only four days a week. This didn't last long, though, as they have changed their calendar to correspond with the Georgian calendar. Now there are four weeks a month and each week is seven days. They use this calendar for a business, while the older version is dedicated to the Orishas.

The Days of the Yoruba Calendar

The four days in the traditional Yoruba calendar are dedicated to different Orishas:

- **Day 1** is dedicated to Orisha Obatala, the father of the sky, Sopona (god of smallpox), Iyami Aje (which means respect), and Egungun (Yoruba masquerade)

- **Day 2** is dedicated to Orunmila, the Orisha of knowledge and wisdom, Esu (trickster god), and Ọṣun, the Orisha of Wisdom

- **Day 3** is dedicated to Ogun, the Orisha of iron and metal, and Oshoshi, the Orisha of hunting
- **Day 4** is dedicated to Sango, the Orisha of lightning, and Oya, his wife, and the Orisha of the weather

The seven days of the updated version that reconciles with the Gregorian calendar are:

Days in English	Days in Yoruba
Sunday	Ojó-Àìkú, the day of immortality
Monday	Ojó-Ajé, the day of economic enterprise
Tuesday	Ojó-Ìségun, the day of victory
Wednesday	Ojó-rú, the day of confusion and disruption
Thursday	Ojó-Bò, the day of arrival
Friday	Ojó-Etì, the day of postponement and delay
Saturday	Ojó-Àbámeta, the day of the three suggestions

The Months of the Yoruba Calendar

June

The first month in the Yoruba calendar is Òkùdú which is June in the Gregorian calendar. The third day of the Òkùdú is the Yoruba new year which is celebrated the same way the rest of the world celebrates the New Year with music, singing, and dancing. There are several Orishas who are celebrated and venerated during this month.

- **Oshosi**, the Orisha of hunting, is celebrated on June 6th
- **Eleguá**, the Orisha of roads, is celebrated on June 13th

- **Ọṣun**, the guardian of Ọrunmila and the Orisha of Wisdom, is celebrated on June 24th

- **Oggún**, the Orisha of iron is celebrated on June 29th

July

The second month in the Yoruba calendar is Agẹmọ. There are three Orishas who are celebrated in Agẹmọ.

- **Aggayú Solá**, the Orisha of volcanoes, is celebrated on July 25th

- **Oke**, the Orisha of the mountains, is celebrated on July 25th

- **Nana Buruku**, the Supreme Goddess, is celebrated on July 26th

August

The third month is named after the Orisha of iron, Ogun. There are two festivals that are usually celebrated this month; the Osun-Osogbo and the Sango festival.

The Osun-Osogbo festival takes place in Osun State in Nigeria every year. The festival celebrates Osun, the river Orisha, and it lasts for two weeks. Since 2005, the celebrations have taken place at a sacred forest that has the same name as the festival. The people of the town of Osogbo consider August to be the time when they can reunite with the culture of their ancestors, cleanse their city, and celebrate.

Various interesting activities take place in this city, like Iwo Popo, which is a traditional cleansing of their town. Another activity is lighting a 500-year-old 16-point lamp called Ina Oloju Merindinlogun, which lasts for three days. The last activity is the Ibroriade, where they collect the crowns of their city's previous kings. Four people usually lead this festival; the sitting Osogbo king, a group of priestesses, the Yeye Osun, and the Arugba, who is a chosen virgin woman. This festival attracts people from all over the world, like tourists and Osun worshippers.

Now we are going to talk about the Sango festival, which takes place every year at the palace of Oyo's ruler. This place honors the god of thunder and iron, Sango. According to legends, Sango was the one who founded the Oyo state boundaries. The festival lasts for a week, and thousands of people from all over the world come to enjoy the celebrations. The festival is considered a tourism and cultural event that UNESCO recognizes. It is also celebrated in many other countries.

In 2013, the Oyo government changed the name of the Sango festival to the World Sango festival.

September

This month is called the Ọwẹ́wẹ̀ in the Yoruba calendar. There are four Orishas that are celebrated and venerated during this month.

- **Yemaya**, the Orisha of the surface of the ocean, is celebrated on September 7th

- **Oshun**, the Orisha river, is celebrated on September 8th

- **Obàtálá**, the creator of human beings and the father of the sky, is celebrated on September t 24th

- **Ibeyis**, the protective twin's Orisha, is celebrated on September 26th

One of the festivals during September is the Olojo festival. It is usually celebrated in Ife town in Osun, and it celebrates Ogun, the Orisha of iron. The people of Yoruba consider Ife to be their city of origin. According to the legends of Yoruba, Ogun is Oduduwa, the creator, first son. The Yoruba people believe they descended from Oduduwa. The word Olojo means "owner of the day," and it is believed that the creator has blessed this day. The Ife king, the Ooni, is usually secluded for a few days before appearing in public on this special day wearing the Are crown, which is the king's crown.

On the day of the festival, the king visits various shrines where he prays for Nigeria and the Yoruba lands to live in peace. This festival celebrates the unification of the people of Yoruba, which is why they hold it in very high esteem.

Another festival celebrated in September is the Igogo festival. This festival is usually celebrated in Owo, an ancient city in Ondo State. Once upon a time, the ruler of Owo was Olowo Rerengejen; he married Orosen, a goddess who became a queen and is honored every year in the Igogo festival.

The Igogo festival is celebrated for 17 days. The celebrations are quite unique and interesting. Since they are honoring a Goddess and a queen, the Owo king and his high chiefs all dress in women's clothes – like gowns. People also celebrate new yams during this festival, commemorating culture and life. It also marks the beginning and end of the farming season.

October

October is called Ọ̀wàrà in the Yoruba culture. There are three Orishas who are celebrated and revered during this month.

- **Orula**, the protector of divination, is celebrated on October 4th
- **Oya**, the mistress of the rainbow, is celebrated on October 15th
- **Inle**, the god of health, is celebrated on October 24th

November

This month is called Bélú. There aren't any Yoruba celebrations or festivals that take place in November.

December

December is called Ọpẹ́. There are two Orishas celebrated and venerated during this month.

- **Shango**, the Orisha of lighting, is celebrated on December 4th
- **Babalú Aye**, the healing Orisha, is celebrated on December 17th

January

The first month in the Gregorian calendar is called Ṣẹ̀rẹ́ in the Yoruba language. There are two Orishas celebrated during this month.

- **Eleguá**, the Orisha of roads, is celebrated on January 6th
- **Osain**, the Orisha of nature, is celebrated on January 17th

February

This month is called Èrèlè in the Yoruba calendar, and there is only one Orisha celebrated during this month.

- **Oya**, the Orisha of the weather is celebrated on February 2nd

The Eyo festival is the only one celebrated in February and is one of the most popular festivals in the Yoruba culture. It takes place every year in Lagos state. During the celebrations, costumed dancers called *Eyo* to come out to perform. *Eyo* means the tall Eyo masquerades, and an interesting fact about this celebration is that these masquerades only allow *tall people* to participate. There are certain rules to this festival; for instance, no one is allowed to wear any footwear, and a popular Yorubian hairstyle known as Suku is prohibited. However, the festival had a very different beginning; it was held to bid farewell to a departed Lagos king and welcome a new one.

There aren't as many followers of the Yoruba religions as there used to be because many followers have converted to Christianity or Islam. However, the Eyo festival is more popular than ever and is considered a huge tourist attraction. One of the reasons behind Eyo's popularity is the masquerade dancers that attract tourists worldwide. It is no wonder why the Lagos government holds this festival in very high regard. Since it attracts tourists from all over the world, this festival help boosts the state's economy, and small businesses benefit so much from it as well.

March

March is called Ẹrẹ̀nà in the Yoruba language. There aren't any Orisha celebrations or Yoruba festivals during this month.

April

April is called the Ìgbé, and only one Orisha is venerated in this month.

- **Yewa**, the Orisha of virginity, is celebrated on April 27th

There is only one festival celebrated in April: the Lagos Black Heritage Festival. It is one of the biggest and most important festivals, and it takes place in Lagos State. It is an annual colorful folk festival.

The African culture has a very rich history, and there is no denying that the African people are very proud of their heritage. This is obvious in the celebrations that take place at the Lagos Black Heritage Festival. It is a day when the Nigerian people proudly show the world their diverse culture. They use different events and entertaining activities to showcase their heritage to the world. They dance, play music, perform, display photos, and do many other festive activities. Additionally, the Lagos Island troops dress up in beautiful costumes and walk around town. It is no wonder it is considered one of the biggest Yoruba celebrations.

May

The last month in the Yoruba calendar is Ẹ̀bìbì. There are two Orishas celebrated in May.

- **Oko**, the Orisha of farming is celebrated on May 15th

- **Oba**, the Orisha of the rivers, is celebrated on May 22nd

The people of Yoruba celebrate the Oro festival in May. Unlike the other festivals usually celebrated in one town or state, this festival takes place in all the Yoruba towns in Nigeria. It is an annual festival with a very unique rule: Only certain people are allowed to participate in the festivities; they must be men or boys, and their fathers must be natives. So, what do the rest of the town's residents do during the festival? According to the rules, all women and non-natives must stay in their homes.

This ancient rule considers it taboo for anyone other than the male paternal natives to see Oro. Since this festival occurs in different towns, you'll find that each one has its own celebrations and traditions. In addition to being an annual festival, the Oro festival is also held when a Yoruba king passes away.

The last festival that we will discuss in this chapter is the Ojude Oba festival which doesn't occur in a specific month. It takes place three days after Eid Al Kabir, or as it is also called Eid Al Adha, a Muslim holiday honoring Ibrahim's willingness to sacrifice his son Ismael.

The Ojude Oba is another annual festival that takes place in Ijebu Ode in Ogun state. There are various activities that take place during this festival, and their purpose is to showcase their history with various entertaining events that focus on their legends and diversity. One of the most important events that take place during this festival is showing allegiance to the king. Wherever the town's natives reside in the country, they must travel to the town's king to show their respect. This festival is very popular since thousands of people attend it every year from all over the country. In addition to these festivals, the people of Nigeria also celebrate traditional holidays like Christmas, New Year, Easter, and two of the most popular Muslim holidays, Eid El Fitr and Eid El Adha.

The Yoruba culture is rich in its language, religion, and legends, and its festivals are as colorful and reflect its magic. The Yoruba people still hold on to their ancient traditions, which they proudly showcase during their festivals. Although these celebrations are all interesting with fascinating history, they are also a huge tourist attraction and boost the country's economy. While customs and traditions have become a thing of the past in many cultures, it is refreshing to see how the people of Yoruba keep theirs alive by celebrating their gods, Orishas, history, and heritage every year. One can understand why the rest of the world is still curious and fascinated with the culture of Yoruba.

Chapter 9: Yoruba Spells, Rituals, and Baths

As the title implies, this chapter contains several simple Yoruba spells, rituals, and baths suitable for beginner Yoruba practitioners. They can offer you protection, guidance, prosperity, and much more. Not only that but most of them can also be altered to suit anyone's individual needs and preferences or invoke a different Orisha if needed. Feel free to use them as they are or add your own spin on them by centering them more on your own specific beliefs.

Seven-Day Candle Ritual for Obatala

Calling on Obatala can be helpful when you need to eliminate negativity from your life or communicate your negative feelings towards the outside world. Using a white, Seven-day candle will ensure you acquire purity in mind and body. The addition of other white food will appease Obatala, so he lends you the ashe you need to obtain your goals.

You'll need:

- A piece of white cotton yarn
- Cascarilla – fresh or dry
- Yams
- Coconut shavings
- Milk
- Rice
- A white, Seven-day candle
- A representation of Obatala

Instructions:

1. Organize your altar or sacred space by clearing up anything you won't need for this ritual.

2. Place the white candle and a symbol representing Obatala on your altar.

3. Prepare the white food – rice, milk, coconut, yams – all in separate bowls and place those on the altar as well.

4. If you are using fresh or whole dried cascarilla, tie the plant in a bunch with a piece of white cotton yarn.

5. If you are using chopped dry leaves, spread them around the candle and tie the yarn around the bottom of the candle.

6. When you are ready, light the candle, close your eyes and prepare to call on Obatala.

Then, recite the following spell:

"Oh, great Obatala, please lend me your power,

Send me patience and knowledge.

May I be strong and wise,

So I can pursue my passions.

Help me stay fair and caring,

To treat others with great integrity."

While traditionally, the candle was intended to be left burning seven days and nights, this is not recommended primarily due to safety concerns. And even if you had a way to keep the candle safe at all times, the spell works only if you keep your mind focused on it. So, instead of worrying about potentially burning down your house (which alone will derail your thoughts from channeling your energy towards the spell), you should opt to burn the candle for regular periods of time over seven days. Whenever you have a little time during the day, light the candle, and recite the spell. When you are finished, snuff it out and go about your day, and when you can, relight it once again until it burns out. In addition, the food is supposed to be served raw, but Obatala will also accept your offering if you prepare a dish from all-white food sources.

Fertility Ritual

This traditional Yoruba ritual has been used by young women who want to conceive a child. Apart from this, Oshun may grant you fertility in many other aspects of life, such as art, work, and even cultivating relationships. The colors and seeds of the pumpkin symbolize the power of nature's fertility.

You'll need:

- 1 pumpkin
- 1 yellow candle
- 1 pencil
- 1 brown paper bag
- A representation of the goddess

Instructions:

1. Place the yellow candle in front of the representation of Oshun on your altar and light it.

2. Close your eyes and focus on manifesting your wishes. Saying them out loud often helps.

3. Open your eyes and carve a round opening in the top of the pumpkin.

4. Take the pencil, and write your wishes down on a piece of the paper bag.

5. Place the piece of paper inside the pumpkin, then pour candle wax on top of it.

6. After ensuring the pumpkin has been sealed with the wax, place it over your stomach, repeating your wishes.

7. When you feel your wishes have been heard, take the pumpkin to the nearest water source, and offer it to Oshun.

You may leave the candle burning for a short period after the ritual is completed, but if you leave it unattended, it's best to snuff it out. You can relight the candle any time you want to during the next five days.

A Prosperity Offering

There are several Orishas associated with prosperity. You can choose to invoke the one whose ashe you need the most according to the area of life you want to prosper in. For example, Oshun may grant you spiritual wealth while Olokun will provide material prosperity.

You'll need:

- 5 oranges
- 1 yellow candle
- 1 white plate
- Cinnamon
- Honey
- A representation of an Orisha

Instructions:

1. Place the yellow candle in front of the representation of the Orisha on your altar and light it.

2. Recite your wish out loud to make sure Orisha can hear you.

3. Put the oranges on a white plate and drizzle them with honey.

4. Sprinkle some cinnamon on top of the oranges as well.

5. Leave the oranges and the topping in front of the Orisha beside the candle for five days.

6. When the five days are up, you may throve or put away the candle and dispose of the offering too.

As with the previous ritual, the candle shouldn't be continuously burning for five days. Feel free to blow it out anytime you leave it and light it again when you can supervise it once again. Make sure to use fresh oranges that can stay safely at room temperature until the ritual is completed.

An Offering for Olokun

Offerings are typically made to Olokun around the time of the traditional harvest celebrations. However, they can also be made on any other occasional date throughout the year for different purposes. Regardless of the date, the offering is best performed in the open air so Olokun will witness the symbolic use of the items and know she is needed. You can incorporate this prayer into your regular practice, and you'll be blessed with Olokun`s protection and guidance.

You'll need:

- A representation of Olokun
- A white handkerchief
- Yemaya incense powder
- Charcoal
- Cowrie shells
- Fruit, grains, meat, and other offerings of your choice

Instructions:

1. Spread the white handkerchief on your altar and place the representation of Olokun on top of it.

2. Put the charcoal in a small bowl and pour some incense powder over it.

3. Light the incense, place the shells in a basket, and then make the offering.

4. Light the candle and say the following prayer:

"I praise the queen of the vast waters.

I praise the queen of the waters beyond understanding.

Oh, queen of the Ocean, I will honor you as long as there is water on the Earth.

Let there be calmness in the waters, so they bring peace to my soul.

I respect the ancient ruler of the water kingdom. Ashé, ashé. "

5. Relax your mind by focusing on the candle's flame or closing your eyes and meditating for a couple of minutes.

6. Work on manifesting your wishes until the incense burns out, then thank Olokun for the blessing she may bestow on you.

The Yemaya powder can be substituted for an incense powder of your choice. Your shell basket can also contain different types of shells, such as seashells – to evoke the queen of the water kingdom. If you offer meat, use only the part of an animal you have prepared to eat, as live animal sacrifices aren't recommended.

Ritual Love Bath

While Oshun is the female Orisha typically associated with love, others can help you make your wishes come true in matters of the heart. The white candle will ensure you see clearly, so you don't miss the person intended for you. The use of your favorite perfume will allow the initial attraction to happen.

You'll need:

- 5 sunflowers
- 1 white candle
- 1 bowl
- A representation of the goddess
- Honey
- Cinnamon
- Your favorite perfume

Instructions:

1. Place the white candle in front of the Orisha on your altar and light it.

2. Tell the Orisha about your wish to find love, preferably by saying it out loud.

3. Remove the petals of the sunflower, and place them in a bowl.

4. Drizzle the petals with honey, sprinkle them with cinnamon, and add a few spritzes of your favorite perfume to them.

5. Pour some water on top of the ingredients in the bowl.

6. Take a shower or a bath, and pour the contents of the bowl over your body. Start from your neck, and move towards your feet.

7. Close your eyes and repeat your wishes once again.

Once again, the candle should be lit for shorter or longer periods of supervised time for five consecutive days. However, the bath ritual itself is only to be repeated once every two to three weeks to leave enough time for love to come into your life.

Sour Bath

This bath aims to acknowledge that while your current life experiences are bitter ones, they can be overturned. Immersing yourself in a sour bath allows you to recognize the negativity around you and change things to work more in your favor. The bitter herbs help with seeing that you aren't the only one with negative experiences. The seven drops of ammonia represent the seven evil forces in Yoruba cultures.

You'll need:

- A pair of tea light candles

- Flowers with red or purple petals

- Fresh or dried bitter herbs, such as yarrow, stinging nettle, horehound, dandelion, and wormwood,

- A half-cup of vinegar – white, red, or apple cider

- Seven drops of ammonia

- An empty cup

Instructions:

1. Around sunset, fill up your bathtub with hot water. Make sure to adjust the temperature to your usual preferences.

2. While the bathtub fills, place the tea light candles around its rim and light them.

3. When the tub has been filled to the desired level, turn off all the electric lights in the bathroom.

4. Toss all the ingredients into the water, then enter the tub between two candles placed opposite each other.

5. Immerse yourself in the water, inhale the bitter scent of the herbs, and focus on the aspects of your life you want to change.

6. You may also pray to the Orishas you use as a guide and ask for their assistance in resolving your problems.

7. Occasional, you should immerse yourself completely in the water. The aim is to spend a total of seven minutes with your head underwater during the course of the bath.

8. Once you feel the water has begun to cool off, you should exit the tub through the gap between the same candle you have entered.

9. Start draining the water – but before it disappears, scoop some of it into the cup along with the ingredients.

10. Don't towel dry unless it's absolutely necessary – let yourself dry naturally instead so the effect of the herbs can soak into your skin.

11. Once you are dry, put on some dark clothes, and take the cup with the bathwater outside.

12. Stand facing west, and hold the cup over your head while saying:

> *"Supreme God who knows and sees all, I have given the Orisha their due. I now declare their hold on me strong. As I cast this water where it's needed, so do I cast out all my problems from my head and life. Ashé, ashé!"*

13. Toss out the water from the cup, head back indoors, and spend some time recouping your strength.

14. Make sure you drink lots of room temperature water so you can replenish the fluids you have lost while soaking in hot water.

This bath should be taken once a week, and it's even easier to incorporate into your regular beauty and healthcare practice than the previous one. Once again, if you want to avoid clogging up your drain while taking this bath, place the herbs into tea bags or organza bags. After your bath, you can spend the time with your normal health care regime, applying shea butter or other natural moisturizing agents, journaling, or meditating. You may also add prayers of gratitude to the Orishas or a deity of your choice. To maximize the ritual's therapeutic effects and ensure a restful sleep, avoid watching TV or using other electronic devices after your bath.

Sweet Bath

While the sour bath allows you to relieve your body of toxins and negative energy at sunset, the sweet one has the purpose of purifying and energizing you at sunrise. The ingredients such as milk, eggs, and honey will nourish your body and revitalize your mind anytime you feel the need for a little pampering.

You'll need:

- A pair of tea light candles
- Flowers with all-white petals such as lilies, roses, daisies, or white chrysanthemums
- Five different fresh or dried healing herbs such as rue, allspice, comfrey, angelica, and hyssop
- A small bottle or jar of honey
- 3 cups of milk
- Powdered cinnamon
- Powdered nutmeg and whole nutmegs
- 1 raw egg
- Your favorite perfume
- An empty cup
- Cocoa butter or shea butter – optional

Instructions:

1. Around sunrise, fill up your bathtub with hot water. Make sure to adjust the temperature to your usual preferences.

2. While the bathtub fills, place the tea light candles around its rim and light them.

3. When the tub has been filled to the desired level, turn off all the electric lights in the bathroom.

4. Crack the egg and toss it in the water. Don't worry if it starts to cook a little bit.

5. Throw on the flowers, herbs, cinnamon, and nutmeg, then follow it with the milk and the honey.

6. Finally, add a few drops of your favorite cologne to the water, then enter it through the gap between two candles as instructed in

the previous ritual.

7. Immersing yourself in the water, and inhaling the sweet scent of the ingredients, focus on the good things that are already in your life. Think about good experiences that way for you on that day and be open to them.

8. You may also express your gratitude to the Orishas for the blessing you may receive on that day.

9. Make sure to immerse yourself fully for a total of final times during your bath.

10. Once you feel the water has begun to cool off, you should exit the tub through the gap between the same candle you have entered.

11. Start draining the water – but before it disappears, scoop some of it into the cup along with the ingredients.

12. Don't towel dry unless it's absolutely necessary – let yourself dry naturally instead so the effect of the herbs can soak into your skin.

13. Once you are dry, put on some light-colored clothes, and take the cup with the bathwater outside.

14. Stand facing east, and hold the cup over your head while saying:

> *"Supreme God who knows and sees all, I welcome with open arms all the beautiful things in life that are waiting for me on my journey! As I cast this water where it's needed, may it serve as an invitation for Oshun so she can bless me with health, love, prosperity, and happiness! Ashé, ashé!"*

15. Toss out the water, head back inside and get ready to welcome the blessings you've invoked.

This bath should be taken once a week, like the previous one incorporated into your regular beauty and healthcare practice. Once again, if you want to avoid clogging up your drain while taking this bath, place the herbs into tea bags or organza bags. While you may not have time to meditate, journey, or perform any other self-care routine before heading out for the day, it's good to avoid using technology and stressful situations right after your bath.

Chapter 10: How Yoruba Influenced Santeria and Others

The Yoruba religion has significantly impacted the new world African diaspora, and it has led to the emergence of belief systems in countries such as Cuba (Santería/ Lucumí, Palo) and Brazil (Umbanda, Candomblé). It also connects with other less-known religions like Haiti (Vodou) and New Orleans (Voodoo/Voudou). This chapter explains how Yoruba religion has managed to influence these African diaspora religions. It also provides details about the similarities and differences between Yoruba and other religions.

Santería

Santeria was brought to Cuba by people from Yoruban countries in West Africa. These individuals were enslaved in the 19th century, but they managed to preserve their religion against the odds. Santeria is a Spanish name that means "The Way of the Saints" and is also known as La Regla de Ocha, meaning "The Order of the Orishas." La Religion Lucumi refers to "The Odu of Lucumi," and is the most popular name associated with religious traditions with origins from Africa and later developed in Cuba and spread to Latin America and the United States.

Santeria is mainly concerned about developing relationships through divination, initiation, sacrifice, and mediumship between the practitioners of the tradition and orisha deities. The main role of deities is to provide wisdom, success, guidance, and protection to the practitioners of the religion during difficult times. A trained priest in the Ifa oracle interprets and provides answers to the questions asked by the devotees. Offerings are presented during ceremonial exchanges, and this practice has since spread to Cuba and other Latin American countries.

Cuba is one of the few countries that received the greatest number of enslaved people from diverse African groups. During the slave trade, more than 700,000 people were enslaved from western Africa – and their final destination was Cuba. Due to the size of the African slaves, their religion of Yoruba continued to thrive even when the slave trade was abolished. The deities with Yoruba origins from Nigeria, Benin, and Togo are called Oricha or Orishas in Spanish. In Cuba and Haiti, the West African deities were paired with Roman Catholic saints, and the religious practice became known as Santeria, referring to "the way of the saints."

Many people are turning against this word since it undermines their religion and the legacy they inherited from their ancestors. Others within the Afro-Caribbean tradition refer to it as La Regla de Lukumi or "the order of Lukumi." Lukumi refers to "my friend," and it comes from the Yoruba greeting.

Following the outbreak of the Cuban revolution in the twentieth century, more than one million Cubans migrated to other cities in the United States. Most people with Yoruban roots moved to Miami and New York, and they later spread their religion to other places. The religion also spread to other cultures like Latinos, African Americans, and even the whites. Many people consulted orishas in the US.

The Cuban immigrants brought Ocha to the US characterized by selling herbs, religious articles, images of the tradition, and candles. While there is no visible public infrastructure, it is believed that between 250,000 and one million people practice this new religion brought by the diasporas in their home temples.

The Orisha tradition has received recognition in different parts of the United States. For example, in 1993, the US Supreme Court allowed the orisha devotees to use animal sacrifices as part of their rites in the case of *Church of the Lukumi Babalu Aye v. City of Hialeah.* Orisha tradition is also portrayed through music, paintings, art, literature, and sculpting. It is likely to continue growing to become a renowned religion across the globe.

Candomblé

Candomblé, like other Afro-Caribbean religions, was brought to Brazil by African slaves between 1549 and 1888. When it emerged in Brazil, it exhibited the characteristics of African cultures, such as Yoruba and other traditions practiced by the Bantu and Fon. Despite being criminalized by other governments and banned by the Catholic Church, the religion thrived for about four centuries. Today, it is an established religion with followers from various social classes and several temples.

About two million Brazilians believe in Candomble religions. Elements like Candomble rituals, deities, and holidays are recognized as part of Brazilian folklore. Candomble refers to a dance meant to honor the gods. Music and dance often accompany many ceremonies and rituals. Most of these traditions are passed orally. Candomblé is practiced by more than two million people in different countries across the globe.

The Candomblé tradition worships the same deities as the Yoruba religion, and it also emphasizes that there is only one supreme creator known as Oludumaré. The intermediaries between the Oludumaré and people are known as orixas. There are also those who function as spirits, and they serve Oludumaré. All individuals are believed to originate from orixa and represent certain foods, colors, and other elements of nature. In Brazil, the spirits that are not deemed as deities are called "Baba Egum." When the devotees are performing a ritual, a priest will dress like the ancestor they want to summon. The women should be part of every ceremony since they will perform dances throughout the ceremony.

Sacred services are usually done in a temple, and some people practice the rituals in sacred places in their homes. Many people were compelled to convert to Catholicism once shipped from West Africa. This led to the protection of the Candomblé religion, which has roots in Yoruba. Candomblé was later condemned since it conflicted with the Catholic religion.

Umbanda

Umbanda is a religion born in Southern Brazil, and it combines Brazilian religion with African traditions, spiritism, and Catholicism. Being exposed to several different religions, such as Yoruba and Catholicism, led to the formation of a new syncretic religion.

Umbanda's formation was quite slow in the 19th century and was later officially recognized in Rio de Janeiro during the 20th century. It was found by Zélio Fernandino de Moraes who was a psychic. He was mainly influenced by spiritualist teachings that led him to create this Umbanda religion. According to the doctrine of spiritism, the souls of all the living things are immortal. The spirits of the dead can assist the living with worldly problems. Umbanda became more prominent in Brazil around the 1930s. This religious system acquired more structural elements from other religions like Yoruba and Catholicism.

There are several mainstream beliefs though there is no uniformity concerning Umbanda religion. Worship is usually done in backyard temples, and this is where many people gathered in the early days. The Umbanda religion's supreme deity is Zambi or Olorun. The orixas are the divine gods that reflect a connection between Zambi and humans. Each Oricha represents different things like justice, love, or protection.

Vodou

Vodou (or Vodoun) is a religion with traceable roots in African traditions which date back to about 6,000 years. Slaves forcibly shipped from Africa brought this religion to Haiti and other islands found in the West Indies. Vodou's birth resulted from a mixture of different cultures like the African religions and Catholic principles in Haiti. A massive number of Africans were transported to the island as slaves, but their large numbers helped them maintain their religion.

Just like the Yoruba cosmology, Voudou's origins also speak of one supreme god known as the Bondye. The believers of this god are convinced that he is the one who created the universe and is also responsible for overseeing human life. Some intermediaries act between this god and the devotees. These can be ancestors or Iwa who are equivalent to Orishas. The Iwa can be divided into two categories based on the African religion, and the following are the most significant.

- **Rada Iwa** – These are benevolent, wise, and helpful spirits gifted with perfume and candy, and they have their origins in Nigeria.

- **Petwa Iwa** – These spirits are malevolent and aggressive, and they are gifted with rum, gunpowder, and firecrackers. They have Congo origins.

Since the Vodou combines various ethnic traits and religious traditions, Iwa was also combined with a Catholic Saint and included the following associations:

- **Damballa/Saint Patrick** – Was perceived as a grandfather figure and also associated with snakes

- **Ogou/Saint George** – A warrior deity who presided over politics, war, and fire.

- **Baron Samedi** – This was the Iwa for the dead, resurrection, and sex. He is known for debauchery and obscenity.

- **Papa Legba/Saint Peter** – The deity is known for being deceptive and persuasive.

- **Erzulie Dantor** – Was later known as the mother of all Haitians and a protector of children.

The Vodou Religion and Haitian Revolution

Between 1791 1ne 1804, the enslaved Africans began to challenge the white plantation owners in Haiti. The slaves were also reorganizing themselves, and the following are some of the things that occurred.

- There were about 250 000 slaves from Africa in the colony

- Only 25 000 white settlers ruled the slaves

- Boukman and Mandal, two prominent Vodou priests and slaves, became the face of the early revolution.

- Vodou was not recorded in text; therefore, masters could not determine what was being planned. Religion was used as a group conscience.

- Vodou ceremonies, such as sacrifices, were performed, and it was believed that religion played a role in the ensuing victory.

- The French were overthrown in 1804, allowing Haiti to become the first colony ruled by slaves.

- Haiti was economically isolated to avoid more revolts, and the Catholic clergy fled and resurfaced around 196, which led to the mixture of the Vodou religion and Catholic motifs without controversy.

- The presence of Catholicism in Haiti led to the persecution of Vodou followers. They were believed to use superstition and other satanic rituals such as cannibalism. All the persecutions were carried out under the 1896 Anti-Superstition Campaign.

- While the persecution later ceased, Vodou is still seen as a sign of backward digression in other parts of the world.

Vodou Rituals and Practices

Vodou rituals are performed in the temple, also known as an ounfo. People will draw veves on the temple walls, and they relate to a particular Iwa.

- When rituals are in progress, an Iwa will possess other devotees. The Iwa should be of the opposite sex.

- Trances can last several hours, and the affected person will not remember anything after coming out of the trance

- Vodou practitioners are called Vodouisants, and the priests are known as mambos and oungans. They assisted people through divination in different problems.

- Vodou culture is associated with negative perceptions like reanimating the dead into zombies. However, this has not been proved anywhere.

After the Haitian revolution, many refugees from the colony migrated to the United States of America to find a new life for themselves. In doing so, they carried their cultural and religious traditions. Vodou and other American religions have been blended, and the Vodou culture is practiced in different areas in the US, such as New Orleans. The increased number of black refugees traveling to the US in the 19th century led to an increase in the Vodou belief system in Louisiana and other Southern states.

Afro-Caribbean and Vodou now include other components of Christianity and American religion. Christian ministers around New Orleans now include some of the Vodou traditions in their sermons since this religion is becoming popular. The leaders of this religion, also known as Voodoo Kings and Queens, were renowned as political figures.

For example, Dr. John, known as Bayou John, is still a famous Voodoo king of New Orleans today. After being born in Senegal, John Bayaou was taken to Cuba as a slave. He settled in New Orleans and was an active member of the Vodou community. His popularity grew since he was reputable for healing and fortune-telling. Another popular figure is Marie Laveau, who became a legend in Voodoo culture in New Orleans. Dr. John was Marie Laveau's mentor. She helped a l0t of enslaved people and attended mass regularly as she was a dedicated Catholic. Vodou religion continues to evolve in the US since many people with African origins still believe in their culture.

The Yoruba religion has led to the emergence of different belief systems, such as in Cuba (Santería/ Lucumí, Palo) and Brazil (Umbanda, Candomblé). It is also connected to other less-known religions like Vodou in Haiti and Voodoo in New Orleans. We have discussed how the Yoruba religion has influenced various African Diaspora religions. Yoruba is recognized as a religion to reckon with in many parts of the world.

Supreme Deities Bonus: Orisha Offerings Cheat Sheet

Suppose you're new to the world of Yoruba. In that case, the chances are that you find it challenging to remember all the Orisha and differentiate between them. Fortunately, you can refer to this bonus cheat sheet whenever you need a quick recap on the various Orisha, their symbols, and their appropriate offerings.

Supreme Deities

Orisha	Symbols and Roles	Appropriate Offering
Olodumare	The supreme creator	Olodumare is worshiped through the other Orishas, which is why he has no shrine or image, and no sacrifices or offerings are made directly to him.
	Not bound by a certain gender	He is not involved in humanity, at least directly, which is why he isn't worshiped.

		He created the concept of delegating	Some people choose to worship Olodumare directly, especially the priests.
		He created the orishas, who are considered intermediary spirits or deities.	The priests give offerings and pray to him; however, little is known about that subject.
		Each orisha has a certain role and dominates a specific area of life.	
		The supreme creator is omnipotent.	
		He isn't directly involved in mundane issues and lets the other Orishas handle earthly matters instead.	
Olórun		The ruler of the heavens.	Since Olorun is a manifestation of Olodumare, he, too, isn't directly worshiped.
		He is a manifestation of the supreme creator or Olodumare	He is aloof, distant, and isn't at all involved in human life.
			Olorun doesn't have any shrines and can't really accept sacrifices or offerings.

		If you wish to offer him, you can send him prayers.
Olofi	Olofi is yet another manifestation of Olodumare.	You can't directly worship Olofi nor send him offerings.
	He is considered the conduit between heaven and Earth, or Orún and Ayé, respectively.	
Nana Buluku	The female supreme deity	Mandrakes
	The root ancestress	Roses
	She is a severe spirit- the witch of the old swamp	Swamp plants
	She can't go inside, as she is too volatile	Other root plants
	The mother of Mawu, the spirit of the Moon, and Lisa, the spirit of the Sun.	
	She is also the mother of the entire universe.	
	She rules the primeval swamp that she is believed to emerge out of.	
	Associations: marches, swamps, clay, and mood	

	Nana Buluku is a divine herbalist. She is the patron of medicinal plants.	
	She has medicinal and magical powers that she can use to heal the ill. She can cure the diseases that medical professionals are unable to identify, locate, or heal.	
	When angered, she can bring about illnesses, especially those with swollen abdomens.	
	Symbols: staffs made of palm fonds and decorated using cowrie shells.	
	Trees: camwood or African sandalwood	
	Stone: tourmaline	
	Colors: black, pink, dark blue, and white	
	Sacred numbers: 7 and 9	

Olodumare and his manifestations aren't directly worshiped because they're too abstract of a concept. It is debated that humans can't grasp the significance of Olodumare as an entity, as he is the most complex spiritual being there is. According to the Yoruba religion, Olodumare, Olorun, and Olofi are incredibly immense beings that are way too immense for the human mind to comprehend. This is why the supreme deity is better broken down into multiple entities that can each exert dominion over particular aspects of life.

Female Orishas

Orisha	Symbols and Roles	Appropriate Offering
Aja	Aja is also known as the wild wind	Aja is a minor Yoruba deity, which is why there isn't much information on how to honor her or what to use as an offering to her.
	She is an orisha and the spirit of herbal healers, the forest, and the animal.	However, we believe that educating others and sharing your knowledge can be a good way to honor the deity.
	She was a herbal healer herself. She mixed the roots and herbs of multiple plants to find cures for those who were sick.	
	She liked to share her knowledge with people who were keen on learning	
	Aja was believed to be a shaman in training.	

	It is said that those who received the education of Aja came back as a Babalawo.	
	She is believed to be one of the rarest Earth gods, and that is perhaps why so little is known about her.	
	She was considered one of the first female doctors of Ocha.	
	She uses the harp, which she has mastered, to convey her messages.	
Aje	Orisha of trade, cash, and wealth	Aje is a minor deity, which is why little is known about her preferred offerings.
	Manifests in both male and female forms	There isn't a specific material element that you can offer to Aje.
	Symbols: tiger cowrie shell	However, you can live by these three principles in her honor: 1. Share everything you have 2. Don't speak about your wealth or display it

		3. Don't use herbs or mess with herbalism without having sufficient knowledge about it. You should also use divine authorization.
	Associations: favors, blessings, and protection	You can recite poems about her
	Dominance: wealth and financial stability	
	Color: white	
Ayao	Orisha of the whirlwind	Ayao is a minor deity, which is why there isn't a lot of information on what should be offered to Ayao. However, you can throw a banquet in her honor.
	Associations: magical knowledge and witchcraft	
	Patron of botanicals and mystical knowledge, which she adopted from being closely acquainted with Osain, the orisha of plants.	
	Symbol: crossbow	
	Colors: green and brown	
	Sacred number: 9	
	Lives in the clouds in the sky, the eye of the tornado, and the forest	

Egungun-Oya	Orisha of divination	Food and gifts can be offered to her and the dead,
	Associations: death, ghosts, destiny, truth, divination, and foresight.	Hang pictures of your loved ones who have passed away and light a candle.
	Mother of the dead	Watch the flame. If it burns out quickly without your interference, you're probably biting off more than you can chew. If the blame burns steadily and brightly, longevity and health are coming in for you. Blue flames that are average-sized suggest that you are in the company of spirits and that you'll live the average life-span.
	Mistress of spiritual destinies	To get rid of unwanted spirits, bring the candle to any light source (like a window) and ask the deity to guide the ghosts out of your house.
	Ruler of fate	
	Symbols: fire and dance	
	She can protect you from the spirits	
Mawu	Continuer of creation	It's not exactly clear what you can offer Mawu the Orisha

	The secondary creator and daughter of Nana Buluku		However, many people recite positive affirmations in honor of the deity.
	Associations: sun, moon, creativity, passion, universal law, birth, inspiration, and abundance		You can recite affirmations on happiness, love, healing, strength, joy, and empowerment.
	Symbols: the moon and clay		
Ọbà	Spirit of the river	Candles	
	Associations: love, faithful wives, neglected women	Flowers	
	Symbols: the sword of the machete, water buffalo, lightning, the flywhisk	Wine	
	Element: water	Lake water	
	Colors: white, pink, and red	Pond water	
		Avoid offering her rainwater or spring water.	
		You can cook beans for her.	

Olókun	Orisha of the sea	Saltwater
	Spirit of life and death	Seashells
	Dominance: fertility, abundance, prosperity, health, and healing	Other marine elements
	Associations: wealth, water, and health	
	Element: water	
	Colors: coral green, dark blue, and red	
	Sacred number: 7	
Ọ̀ṣun	Spirit of sweet water	Mirrors, makeup, perfume, brushes, and all other things related to feminine beauty
	Dominance: honey, love, water, mother's milk, and money	Fans made of peacock feathers
	Sacred number: 5	Yellow sandalwood fans
	Associations: love, beauty, wealth, romance, magic, and abundance	Flowers
	Symbol: a pot that contains river water	Chamomile tea

	Colors: all the shades of yellow, orange, and gold	Spinach with shrimp
	Plants: marigold, lantana, yellow squash, pumpkins, and rosemary	Honey- make sure to open the jar and taste the honey before you offer it to her. Someone had previously attempted to poison Osun through a honey offering. She will reject your offering of honey if you don't taste it first.
	Jewels: coral and amber	Orange and yellow fruit
		Orange and yellow vegetables
Ọya	Orisha of the wind, violent storms, and lighting	Purple plums
	Guardian of the gates of death	Starfruit
	She doesn't represent death. She is representative of air	Black grapes
	Master of disguise, especially as a buffalo	Purple grapes
	Associations: rebirth and death	Black-eyed peas

	Symbols: lightning bolt, thunderbolt, buffalo, wind, tornadoes, and fire	Nine eggplants- you can also slice one eggplant into nine pieces.
	Colors: maroon	Meals that incorporate eggplants- are typically served with nine-bean soup and rice.
	Sacred number: 9	Red wine
	Metal: copper	The offerings can be presented at a home altar or the cemetery gates.
	Tree: camwood and akoko	
	Plants: cypress, camphor, marigold, flamboyant, and mimosa	
Yemoja	Queen of the Sea The mother of most of the Orishas Dominance: reproductive and fertility problems, domestic violence protection, sea travel Associations: women and children, benevolence, generosity Symbols: seashells and other marine symbols Colors: white and blue Sacred number: 7	Jewelry Perfume Scented soap. It must be new and unwrapped Flowers, particularly white roses Pomegranates, watermelon, and other wet and seedy fruits Pork cracklins Banana chips Plantain chips Poundcake Coconut cake

| | Plants: water hyacinth, seaweed, and indigo | Drizzle molasses over everything |
| | Crystals and minerals: coral, quartz crystals, and pearls | Sea creatures |

Male Orishas

Orisha	Symbols and Roles	Appropriate Offering
Aganjú	Spirit of the forces of the Earth, especially those that are powerful and violent	Nine crackers and red palm oil
	Orisha of Volcanoes	Nine fruits
	Associations: transportation and travel. His displeasure is associated with aneurysms, traffic accidents, sudden strokes, and high blood pressure	Nine plantains served with red palm oil
	Color: red	Nine handkerchiefs
	Sacred numbers: 9 and 16	Nine silk pockets
		The handkerchiefs and silk pockets must be folded in squares. Each one should be in a different solid color.

Babalú Ayé	Father of the Earth	Roasted corn
	The spirit of smallpox and disease- he protects against the disease he represents	Popcorn
	He represents the ailment and its vaccine	Sesame seeds
	Dominance: minor and major skin ailments, infections, and diseases.	Cookies
	Associations: death, cemeteries, diseases.	Candy
	Sacred Number: 17	Cigars
	Colors: vary according to tradition- white, brown, black, red, yellow, and purple	Cowrie shells
	Plant: cactus	Babalu drinks
	Tree: Odan	Fine white wine
		Chicken
		If you're seeking him for healing, offer him Milagros (small religious folk charms). If he answers, offer more
		Don't offer water

Erinlẹ̀	Orisha of fertility, abundance, and wealth	Tiny metal charms in the shape of fish
	Spirit of the bush	Images of sparkly fish
	Underwater king	Images of sparkly fish
	Sacred number: 7	Swedish fish candy
	Symbols: cowries, fishing rods, and bows and arrows	
	Associations: Earth, the universe and its natural laws, hunting, and wealth	
	Colors: turquoise, indigo, coral	
	Mineral: Gold	
Èṣù	God of roads, especially crossroads	Candy
	Protector of travelers	Rum
	Dominance: fortune and misfortune, and divine law	Toys
	Colors: red and black	Spicy food
	Sacred number: 3	Cigarettes

	Symbols: crutches, canes, cross, and key	Food with peppers and hot sauce
	Tree: calabash	
	Plants: seedlings, vira mundo aroma, curujey, guava, guira cimarrona, camphor, cress, and cat's claw scent	
	Associations: natural laws, divine laws, and orderliness	
Ibeji	Representative of pair of twins	Toys
	Orishas of the divine twins	Sweets
	Sacred numbers: 2, 4, and 8	Anything fun
	Colors: red and blue	Fruit
	Associations: mischief, abundance, and joy	Yellow rice
	Symbols: twin dolls	Sugarcane
	They are kids	Black-eyed peas
		Okra

		Drinks and fruit juices
		Things served in pairs
		Small bananas- manzanos
		Cakes
		Chicken and rice
Ọbàtálá	The father of the sky	His diet is bland and restricted.
	The creator of human bodies	Hates salt and spicy food.
	The oldest of all Orishas	Prefers white or light-colored offerings.
	The king of religion in heaven, or Orun	Rice
	Color: white	Coconut
	Sacred number: 8	Eggs
	Dominance: purity	Cocoa butter
	Associations: purpose, peace, honesty, purity, resurrection, the New Year, and forgiveness	White yams
	Symbols: white crown, staff, dove	Meringues

	Plants: acacia, barberry, bell, cotton, atipola, bayonet, scourer, may flower, soursop, and white, mauve.	White sacrifices like hens, female goats, and doves.
Oduduwa	The first king of Oyo	He eats with Obbatala, the white Orisha, and accepts sacrifices like: • White goats • Hens • Guinea pigs • Quails • Pigeons
	The oldest dead man	
	The lord of desires	
	A creator, a justice doer	
	Associations: death, purity, harmony, creation, and energy	
	Colors: white and opal	
Ògún	Primordial Orisha	He will eat just about anything due to his big appetite
	The first king of Ife	Plantains
	The god of war and metals	Jutia (small rodents)
	Dominance: transformation, function, and life	Smoked fish

	Associations: tools, creativity, and intelligence	Pomegranates
	Sacred numbers: 3 and 7	Watermelons
	Colors: red, black, and green	Rum
	Plants: cyperus esculentus, garlic, rosemary, chile pepper, black pepper, and other medicinal herbs	Grapes
	Trees: akoko, camwood, palm, eucalyptus, and calabash	Gin
	Symbols: palm frond, iron, and the dog	Bananas
		Pigeons
		He-goat
		roosters
Oko	The Orisha of agriculture, farming, and fertility	All crops, especially root vegetables
	Dominance: life, earth, and death	Yams

	Associations: health, vitality, and stability	Sweet potatoes
	Colors: red, white, pink, and light blue	Corn
	Sacred number: 7	Taro root
		Palm oil seasoned foods
		Toasted corn
		Smoked fish
Osanyin	The Orisha of nature	Coins
	Healing herbs	Alcohol, especially aguardiente
	Colors: green, red, white, and yellow	Rum
	Sacred numbers: 6, 21, and 7	Candles
	Dominance: forests, herbalism, healing, and wild areas	Tobacco
	Associations: plants, magic, talking, and healing	
	Symbols: twisted tree branches and pipes	
	Multi-colored beads	

Oṣùmàrè	Divine serpent	Corn
	Orisha of the rainbow, transformation, serpent, and cycles	Cowries
		Shrimp sauteed in dende oil
		Beans
	Guardian and protector of children	Pure water
		Roosters and armadillo
	Colors: yellow, purple, burgundy, pink, and green	Peanuts
		Yams
		Sweet potatoes
	Dominance: permeance and wealth	
	Associations: regenerations, transformation, and rebirth	
	Symbols: serpents and rainbows	
	Cowrie shells, iron, yellow, and green glass beads	
Òṣóòsì	The spirits of meals, as he is the provider of food.	He loves to be offered hunted animals, like cooked pigs, guinea fowl, quails, deer, pigeons, and goats.
	Orisha of contemplation and the patron of arts and all things beautiful	Grapes
	Colors: Blue in Ketu and green elsewhere	Pears

	Sacred numbers: 3, 4, and 7	Smoked fish
	Dominance: forests, hunts, wealth, and animals	Plantains
	Associations: craftiness, wisdom, lightness, and astuteness when hunting.	Pomegranates
	Plants: strenna white, scorpionfish, partridge vine, coral, enchantment, coast incense, prodigious, yellow cabin	Bananas
	Symbols: crossbow and arrow	Anisette
		Jutia
		Sweet potato fries
		cigar
Shango	The father of the sky	Rum
	The god of thunder and lightning	Whiskey- some recommend Jack Daniels, in particular.
	Colors: Red, gold, and white	Beer

	Sacred numbers:4 and 6	Tobacco
	Dominance: human vitality and male sexuality	Chili
	Stones: carnelian, fire opals, diamonds, and gold.	Peppers
	Associations: protection, drumming, justice, life, magick, fire, thunder, lightning, and virility.	Hot and spicy food
	Plants: chili peppers, red oak trees, marijuana, hibiscus, chinaberry, and sassafras.	Gunpowder
	Symbols: thunderstorms, red and white bead necklaces, lightning bolts, and double-headed axes.	Meat

There are numerous Yoruba Orishas, each of which rules a certain aspect of life. Each Orisha demands unique offerings and has different characteristics and temperaments. This makes it impossible for most people, especially those new to this belief system, to always remember who is who. Fortunately, you can always refer to this cheat sheet whenever you need to be reminded of the deities and all their aspects.

Conclusion

The Yoruba religion is one of the most fascinating religions in the world. It is filled with legends, myths, and magic. In this book, we have covered everything that you would want to know about the enchanting world of the Ìṣẹ̀ṣe. We have provided information about its history and culture, so you have enough background to start your learning journey. You also learned about Olorun, the Supreme God, and the creation myth.

The world of the Orishas is probably the most interesting part of the Yoruba religion. As the intercessors between humans and the Supreme God, Orishas play a huge role in helping people communicate with Oldorun. To call on the Orishas and take advantage of their powers, you first need to know who they are and how they can help you. All the information to help you navigate their world, including how many Orishas there are – and which are the most helpful and important ones – has been discussed.

All gods prefer offerings and sacrifices, and Orishas are no different. Learning about how you can appease these gods will be beneficial when you call on them to ask for their assistance. There are male and female Orishas, each with a fascinating history and legends behind them. Whether you are sick, want a child, or looking for love, you'll find an Orisha willing to help. As giving as Orishas are, some of them can be angry and destructive, and we have the information you need to navigate your way through the Orishas you should never anger or provoke. Just like people, some Orishas don't get along with each other. Learning about their history will help you avoid venerating rival Orishas together like Oya and Oshun.

In the next part of the book, we talked about the practice of Ifa divination and how it works. You read about the diviner Babalawo and whether anyone can become one. Additionally, we covered the importance of ancestors in the Yoruba religion. We need to honor our ancestors and seek their wisdom to help us navigate life. We talked about venerating them, which usually occurs on an altar. After finishing chapter 7, you'll be ready to create an altar or shrine dedicated to your ancestors.

Every religion has its calendar and holy days. Each day of the week is called something different and has a different meaning in the Yoruba religion. To practice this religion, you need to learn about its various holidays so you can celebrate them with your loved ones. We provided all of the information you need regarding important festivals as well. There are also many Yoruba spells and rituals that you should learn about, and in this book, you'll find all of the ingredients and instructions you need to start practicing.

Yoruba is a religion rich in legends, myths, gods, and magic. It has become a huge influence on other religions all over the world. Now you've learned about many of these other beliefs, what they have in common with Yoruba, and what sets them apart. There is so much about the Yoruba religion out there; we hope we've brought you all of the essential information you'll need to learn about your spiritual heritage. Good luck on your journey!

Part 2: Ifá

The Ultimate Guide to a System of Divination and Religion of the Yoruba People

Introduction

The rich, complex heritage of the Ifá religion has deep roots in the soil of West Africa, in the region known as Yorubaland. Encompassing the three modern states of Nigeria, Benin, and Togo, over 75 percent of Yorubaland is found in Nigeria. With a population numbering 55 million, most residents of Yorubaland are ethnic Yoruba people.

From the Yoruba, Ifá arose, giving birth to religious expressions in the New World. Born across the Atlantic with the enslaved people who built that world on behalf of European colonialism, Ifá is the root of Santeria, Candomblé, Sango Baptism, and Voudon.

Through these New World religions and other spiritual practices arising in the African diaspora, Ifá's cosmology and principle characteristics have been diffused worldwide. While their manifestation in these "spinoffs" is markedly different, the roots remain, ever leading back to the fruitful soil of Mother Africa.

Despite the best efforts of colonialists in Africa to impose the Christian religion, Ifá has not only survived but thrived. New World reflections of Ifá began to migrate north to the United States from countries like Cuba, Haiti, and Brazil, bringing a new interest in an ancient way of worship and life that resonates with the descendants of those taken from the shores of Africa.

At the heart of Ifá is divination, a mediating link between humanity and the spirit world. Drawing on the oral traditions of Odù Ifá and the oral transmission of folk tales and prose from Babalawo (meaning "father of the secrets" or "father of wisdom") to Babalawo through time, divination in Ifá relies on the interpretation of signs provided by the tools of divination. These are used to arrive at the Odù—or narrative from Odù Ifá—which will instruct followers seeking guidance. Interpreted by the Babalawo, divination provides practitioners of Ifá with a way to discern the guidance of the spirit world and the direction in which fate is taking them.

For adherents of Ifá, it is more than a religion. Ifá is a connection to the world of the spirits and their will for individual human life. The folk tales and prose carried by the hallowed Babalawo guide practitioners, serving to draw wisdom from the common scenarios of life for the conduct of their own lives. Ifá is founded on intellectual development—which leads to the perfection of individual lives—and the wisdom of the spirits shared with the living. In that development is the motivation for those who follow the Ifá religion—the soul's journey as an active, intentional consecration of human life to the will of the Divine.

In this book, you will discover a unique religion as old as 8,000 years. A religion that is still practiced to this day. The United Nations Educational Scientific and Cultural Association (UNESCO) named the religion a Masterpiece of Oral and Intangible Heritage of Humanity.

Explore Ifá, its divination practices, and spiritual disciplines. Enter a world guided by the hunger to transcend through ancient mysteries.

Chapter 1: What Is Ifá?

"The song changes, so the drumming changes to suit it." — Yoruba Proverb

The proverb above is a good place to start our journey to the heart of Ifá. Ifá is more than a religion; Ifá is the command center of life. The faithful find meaning, direction, and the abiding comfort of spiritual guidance tethered to the intellect within its embrace.

This is one of Ifá's most striking features. While it is clear that the Near Eastern monotheistic faiths (Judaism, Christianity, and Islam) call on the intellect for those of the clerical class, the laity (those not ordained to the sacramental and/or pastoral service of God) are often called only to believe. The converse is true of Ifá, in which intellectual development is a component of the spirituality of the faithful.

The song in the quote is, of course, life. And, as we all know, the song of life has all kinds of changes. The drumming changes a lot as we move along on the journey. This is the true genius of Ifá. Human beings seeking guidance from the spirits through divination are connected in ritual. More than that, they are engaged intellectually, working with what they learn from the Divine Will.

In this first chapter, you will discover the history of Ifá and learn about the ethnic group it originated from, the Yoruba.

Who Are the Yoruba?

Until 1292 BCE, ancient Egypt was ruled by Nubian pharaohs. At this time—the nineteenth Dynasty—the rule of this ancient monarchy fell into the hands of Eurasian and Arabic monarchs (see the Resources section).

Taharqa, the Nubian Pharoah.

Aidan McRae Thomson, CC BY-SA 2.0 <https://creativecommons.org/licenses/by-sa/2.0>, via Wikimedia Commons https://commons.wikimedia.org/wiki/File:Taharqa_portrait,_Aswan_Nubian_museum.jpg

Migrating from what is now Saudi Arabia, the Biblical "Cushites" arrived in the Nile Valley to establish themselves there and to become a vital part of ancient Egypt, its culture, leadership, and religious expression. After thousands of years, these people were known as the "Yoruba."

The Yoruba worshipped a pantheon of deities as the Cushites of the Arabian Peninsula and brought their system of beliefs with them. As their influence grew as philosophical and spiritual leaders, those beliefs came to be part of the fabric of ancient Egypt's religious framework. In the sophistication and complexity of Egyptian beliefs, the echoes of the Cushites and a foretaste of Ifá can be readily observed.

The oral traditions of the Yoruba recount a migration from ancient Egypt—of which Nubia formed a part—bringing with them the ways of Egypt, refined from the earlier ways of Arabia. The monarchical system of the Yoruba bears a striking resemblance to that of ancient Egypt. However, burial practices and art also speak to this connection. Even today, many Yoruba trace their origins to Egypt and the Nile Valley. While there is much divergence on the part of archaeologists and historians, the Yoruba themselves adhere to this general version of events in establishing what became the Yoruba people in Yorubaland.

But until 1830, the word "Yoruba" was not used to describe these people. The term described a series of ethnic subgroups related by custom, regional origin, and religious practice. These were groups like the Oyo, Ketu, and Egba. The Yoruba were then living in city-states—which still characterize the political organization of today's Yorubaland.

Wandering through the ancient Near East, establishing in Egypt and then moving on again to Nigeria, Togo, and Benin, the Yoruba were dispersed by the Trans-Atlantic Slave Trade. Finally, they culminated in the Yoruba identity in Yorubaland as it is known today and brought a version of Ifá belief to the New World with the enslaved.

Ifá — The Touchstone of Yoruba Life

The word "Ifá" seems not to travel well, like many words in all languages. Boiled down as a central theme, it means an attraction, and in that attraction is the role Ifá plays in Yoruba life.

The attraction in question is to spiritual and material wisdom, simultaneously resulting in an improvement and purification of the practitioner's life. The human intellect is enlisted to work with the interpretations of the father priest, the Babalawo, or Iyalawo, the female priest, concerning divination (which will be discussed later). The result is a combination of lessons received in divination and how the practitioner lives those lessons in real-time.

The church of Ifá is the human being because it is in the human being that the wishes of the spirit world are realized. By learning from the wisdom of the spirits, Ifá practitioners are guided into a life radiant with both spiritual and practical meaning. There is no genuine division between the spirit and the body. In Ifá, they are one, just as the faithful are one with the spirit world through the divination expertise of the learned "father/mother priests."

All that is—living, dead, and yet to be, material and spiritual—is one. In this universal unity with the Divine source is the integrated philosophy of Ifá. It is a religion permeating every corner of the practitioner's life, just as the Divine infuses the Created Order with its numinous presence. There is no genuine division—save for cosmology (which will be discussed shortly). There is only unity. Each human participates in that unity as a planned component of the greater whole.

Ifá, then, is an attraction of the human soul to a Divine blueprint for living. In living as an integral part of a planned construct, the individual is not obligated to participate. Instead, Ifá calls counsel and steers the faithful in the right direction, hoping that the lessons stick. When they do not, an opportunity for more learning presents itself.

Governing all human behavior in Ifá are the Sixteen Commandments of the Faith.

Ifá's Sixteen Commandments (Ika Ofun)

Please note that you will see many versions of the Sixteen Commandments of Ifá online. The translation and personal interpretation play a part in the differences.

These commandments are the pillars of Ifá, fortifying the community with individual integrity that creates a microcosm of wholeness.

1. **Do Not Lie**

   Lying, in Ifá, is viewed as a failure of wisdom, intellect, and spirit. It is, therefore, a shortcoming that will eventually harm the life of the practitioner. The goal of Ifá is to eradicate the urge to lie and replace it with wise responses from lessons learned.

2. **Do Not Practice Ifá Without Understanding**

   Pay special attention to this commandment. Ifá is not a mud puddle for dabblers to splash in. It is an ancient and profound religion and way of life. No aspect of Ifá, including divination, should be approached without understanding and reverence.

3. Do Not Mislead

To mislead is to tell untruths, so the commandment not to mislead addresses the practitioner's duty not to harm the community by steering any member of it in the wrong direction. The associated human cost can be very high.

4. Do Not Cheat

Are you detecting a theme? Dishonesty is such a huge "no-no" in Ifá that three closely related variations are included in its major prescriptions for living. In this instance, cheating refers specifically to money and spirituality.

5. Do Not Pretend to Be Wiser Than You Are

We all know someone who claims to have in-depth knowledge of various subjects but, in truth, knows only the headlines. Ifá directly forbids such vain posturing, counseling that wisdom is attained through the intellect and spirit working together and cannot be feigned.

6. Be Humble

Humility is woven into the fabric of Ifá in the meaning of the word. The attraction of the faithful is to wisdom, intellectual, and spiritual development. To attain these things, the humility of learning how to be a better human being teaches the commandment itself.

7. Do Not Be Sneaky or Treacherous

Sneakiness, betrayal, and manipulation are all hallmarks of disordered, unhappy people. Those who seek to manipulate others, and sneak around behind their backs to sow confusion and discontent, are not living sanctified lives but breaking lives for the ego's sake.

8. Taboos and Superstition Have No Power Over You

Here is where we encounter the practical orientation of Ifá. Taboos and superstitions are primarily cultural, leading to outlandish beliefs that have the power to knock the faithful off their course of sanctified communal living. They contribute nothing to life and should have no influence.

9. Do Not be Arrogant About Taboos and Superstitions

Western societies have plenty of cultural taboos and superstitions. Many of us tend to laugh at them. Ifá prohibits this, and the commandment to be humble precludes any derisive display in their confrontation. Rather, any belief in their power is met with studied neutrality.

10. Be Trustworthy

Being someone that other people can consistently trust is the hallmark of a well-developed person. Having learned the wisdom of the spirits and ancestors, the Ifá adherent does not tell others' secrets and keeps promises.

11. Respect the Challenges of Others

Expressed as the command to not take the cane from the hand of a blind person, this commandment counsels the active support of those with challenges like blindness, mobility issues, deafness, muteness, or any other challenge that makes them vulnerable to the ill will of others. These people are not to be interfered with but supported. All challenges of any kind are viewed as an opportunity to model decency.

12. Respect Your Elders

Near the end of their earthly journeys, older people are unquestioningly respected as those who have gathered wisdom and lessons from Ifá. They are living wisdom and, thus, sacred exemplars.

13. Respect Other People's Marriages/Relationships

Sexual morality means not interfering with the relationships and marriages of others by setting your sights on one of the partners. It also means being sincere with your sexual partners and not misrepresenting yourself.

14. Do Not Sexually Betray a Friend

Of all the marriages and relationships Ifá practitioners should not mess with, their friends' are at the top of the list. Sexually engaging with a friend's wife or husband represents a profound rupture in the integrity of the community.

15. Do Not Betray Secrets

Disseminating information entrusted to you destroys your community standing and the ability of other people to trust you. It provokes cynicism and social isolation.

16. Do Not Disrespect the Priests

The priests of Ifá are in place to guide the community with their knowledge gained from years of training. To disrespect the priests is to disrespect the deposit of oral history and tradition they have been entrusted with and, by extension, to disrespect Ifá itself.

The Role of Divination

Divination is a central ritual focus in Ifá, used to provide the faithful with guidance and growth. This book is largely concerned with this aspect of the Faith, but it is helpful to know what divination is intended to achieve.

Divination's centrality to believers' governance and philosophical framework is its communal strength. It is used for everything from discerning the will of the spirit world for a new year to selecting a new leader, and divination also serves the faithful as a means of both following and shifting their destiny.

Because in Ifá, destiny is written by the Divine, but it's also "plastic." Its malleability is in the willingness of the individual practitioner to take control of what life has in store to change fortune's trajectory. Divination takes the temperature of existing worldly conditions, consults with spirit, and prescribes remedial action. Divination also serves the faithful by reminding them that spirit is in control of all that is and that only through intercession can human beings protect themselves from the vagaries of an uncertain world.

For big and small questions, divination is not a passive process to attract good fortune and protect against bad fortune. The agency of the person approaching the Babalawo/Iyalawo for a reading starts the process. While divination provides answers, it's entirely up to the person seeking the spirit world's guidance to act on those answers. Divination is of little use to the person seeking it without this implied and expected participation.

However, there is a more serious consequence involved when the guidance of divination is not acted upon.

In Heaven, as It Is on Earth

As seen in the Sixteen Commandments of Ifá, this religion and lifestyle are rooted in common decency: Respect for other people, humility, and self-awareness. These qualities describe humanity on its best behavior.

The emphasis on orthopraxy—right action, as opposed to "orthodoxy" or right thinking—points to a functional reason for that emphasis. Simply, what happens on earth does not stay on earth. Rather, what happens on earth has repercussions in the spirit world (heaven).

Thus, for the sake of the integrity of the spirit world, entangled with the material world through the Divine spirit that lives far away in the heavens, divination stands in the gap. The gap, of course, is that of the flesh and its errant ways. Divination teaches the flesh the ways of spirit by divining its wisdom through the agency of priestly expertise and the tools used (which will be discussed later).

When human beings in the community adhere to the perfection of their spirits, they hold up to heaven. This is not only for heaven's sake but also for their own. The world of the spirits is the promise of life's other side, hidden deep within us as our portion. That portion is not genuinely ours. It is a gift of the Divine, not unlike a ticket to the ultimate rave. While through the soul, we are fully integrated with all that is, our flesh must convey us through life's lessons. While the flesh is created and holy, it is also the site of our most damaging human traits. The flesh is where we learn and what we purify in that learning toward the perfection of the spirit.

Divination's central role in Ifá reveals a fundamental truth about this spiritual lifestyle. The unity of all things is impacted by humanity's willingness to examine itself and to seek out the spirit in that examination. In divination, Ifá adds a functional learning tool that feeds the spirit as lessons are absorbed in the flesh. When the flesh is no longer at war with spirit, it has evolved to model more of its potential—but there is an eternity for human potential to develop fully, in Ifá.

The Sixteen Commandments are clear. They proscribe the communally corrosive and prescribe the socially constructive. In demanding individual fidelity to a common standard of virtuous conduct, the Commandments reinforce the integrity of spirit, knitting the Created Order into union with its Divine source. When the good on earth is multiplied, the integrity of heaven is fortified. This unity, in Ifá, is expressed in communal fidelity, which mirrors divinely mandated unity between the Created and the Creator.

Wisdom and Intellect

Ifá is loosely translated as "attraction." That attraction is to the pursuit of wisdom sparked by intellect and touched by the spirit. But wisdom and intellect are not for their own sake in Ifá. They serve a much larger purpose.

That purpose is the ordering of the universe through the orthopraxy of righteous people. This righteousness is not for its own sake, either. Rather, it serves the greater goal, which is the unity and integrity of all. It reserves the resolution of the errant, egotistical ways of the flesh, directing the individual toward the way that serves the community and, thus, the goal.

In Ifá, wisdom and intellect have a divine source, and that is OlOdù mare, the creator deity of Ifá and the source of the Created Order.

In the next chapter, you will meet OlOdù mare, find out about the origin of Ifá divination, and discover the Ifá version of the Creation narrative.

Chapter 2: God and the Great High Priest

OlOdù mare, the name of God in Ifá, has a very familiar profile. To start with, OlOdù mare (also known as Olorun) is called the Lord of Heaven and Creator. Like the God of the Hebrew and Christian Scriptures, OlOdù mare is not a creature but so completely "Other" and ontologically inscrutable that human beings cannot even begin to conceive Their substance.

OlOdù mare is sometimes described as the "Monarch who can't be found, even if you search earnestly." This ineffability and otherness align with the God of the Hebrew Scriptures. They, when quizzed by Moses as to Their name, replied, "I am what I am" (expressed in Hebrew as "YHVH," the Tetragrammaton, Exodus 3:14). This ineffability is similarly emphasized in Ifá's conceptualization of the Divine.

OlOdù mare's story is of a god removed. Once near the Creation wrought by his hand, the God of Ifá became remote yet accessible. Ever near in spirit to Creation, OlOdù mare continued to connect with people and hear their pleas. The similarities—superficially—end between the God of Ifá and the God of the Hebrew and Christian Scriptures. Because, while reachable, OlOdù mare knew they needed an emissary on the ground.

The Ifá Creation Narrative

Long, long ago, Olodumare lived nearer to humanity's home than he does now. There was no question that we were within each other's reach. God was one of us—a neighbor just down the block.

However, then, humanity got arrogant. Humanity began to plunder heaven indiscriminately and disrespectfully, raiding the food of the heavenly precincts and throwing apple cores on the ground. Olodumare was not amused.

Thus, our "neighbor just down the block" packed up and moved further away from us, worn out from yelling, "Get off my lawn!" We know where Olodumare lives and vice versa, but we take each other in small doses, still smarting from that long-ago squabble that came between us.

Before that happened, many interchanges occurred between Olodumare in heaven above and humanity on earth below. This is depicted in Ifá as a swampy wasteland (as in the Biblical Creation narrative where the earth is described as "formless and void" Genesis 1: 2). Thanks to a chain that connected heaven and earth, this interchange occurred, allowing two-way free passage.

Olodumare is in heaven and humanity below.
https://unsplash.com/photos/Fem4uCQ7VEg

Olodumare saw the earth's state, so he instructed Obatala (Ifá's co-creative Orisha, see Chapter Three) to clean it up and make it solid. OlOdù mare gave Obatala the tools to follow his instructions: A snail shell filled with dirt, a pigeon, and a hen.

So, Obatala set off, and when he arrived at the swampy mess the earth was, he threw the dirt from the snail shell and let the pigeon and hen fly off to spread it around. Obatala then commanded a chimera to check on the work of the birds and pronounce its sound.

The chimera reported that the earth still needed more work as parts of it were not yet up to snuff. The chimera then returned for a second inspection, after which he reported to Obatala that the work had been completed.

Obatala returned to OlOdù mare's presence and reported success. OlOdù mare then gave Obatala another commission—equipping the earth with all needed to sustain life. Obatala, deciding this was a big job, took Orunmila (the oracle Orisha) with him as an advisor.

First, the palm tree was created to give food, oil, leaves to build homes with, and the fruit's juice to drink. Then, Obatala received three more fruit-bearing trees for humans to derive juice from, as there was no rain yet. The hen and the pigeon would become the ancestors of all birds.

Olodumare asked Obatala to take sixteen humans he had created in the heavenly precincts to the earth when all this work was completed. Obatala was then instructed to create forms in human shape, as Obatala could not give them life. As the God of Ifá, only Olodumare could give life to the forms. Thus, he did, breathing into their nostrils to animate them. (NB: Another remarkable similarity to the Genesis Creation narrative, see Genesis 2: 7.)

The Origin of Divination

Olodumare asked Orunmila to remain on the earth to counsel the faithful through the medium of divination. As mentioned, divination may be employed to arrive at communal decisions about leadership. For individual practitioners, though, it serves as a touchstone, providing supplicants with valuable information and empowering them to change their lives and destinies by using their intellects and spirits in unison.

In recent times, divination has joined forces with our material world's scientific and intellectual institutions, with the spirits counseling practitioners to seek the help of doctors, lawyers, and other professionals. However, divination stands as a message of OlOdù mare's love for humanity. It provides a means by which the living can seek the counsel of the spirit world, deriving better lives and living more happily and fruitfully in the process.

Divination is a spiritual tool that serves the faithful and the community they live in, dispensing advice, giving answers to questions, and these days, directing them to help professionals to accomplish the leading of the spirit.

Because OlOdù mare moved away from the earth, Orunmila acts as his intermediary, replacing the in situ Divine Presence with that of a proxy, overseeing the conduct of divination and the fitness and expertise of those charged with sharing its gifts, the Babalawo/Iyalawo. It was also Orunmila who established the Ifá's oral tradition, the Odù Ifá. For this, he is known as the High Priest and Revelator of OlOdù mare's divinity and the prophetic gift of divination. (NB: For this purpose, the Biblical interpretation of prophecy is to "reveal." Specifically, prophecy reveals truths that liberate.)

And because divination sprang from the mind of the Creator, OlOdù mare, divination is a sacred center of life for those who practice Ifá. Complex in its practice and a sacred link between the people and their God, divination is that chain between heaven and earth whose links by the Oracle, Orunmila, are strengthened with each lesson learned and acted on.

The Distant God

The retraction of OlOdù mare from the earth is, in truth, the very heart of the need for divination in the Divine mind. Human beings were rude, vulgar, and obnoxious. They needed their Creator, but there is only so much a loving god can handle. OlOdù mare solved the problem of Their anger by moving far enough away from human beings to reduce the temptation to punish them.

Instead, God left an emissary on earth to sort things out. Humanity looked fine, but it was not. The situation demanded a prolonged tweak to set it straight—and that tweak was divination. Through divination, the community of Ifá is ordered toward greater fidelity with the original prototype of humanity. With the support of the learned Babalawo/Iyalawo, divination turned the community's mind to self-development in the service of the Divine-human relationship, weaving it carefully back together in respectful service to something greater than the self.

OlOdù mare is distant from humanity in cosmology but near in the person of Orunmila and the gift of divination. Through Orunmila, the Almighty acts to repair a damaged humanity, void of respect for its

Creator and heaven itself. Returning to the Sixteen Commandments of Ifá in Chapter One, we can see that the Ifá Creation story is the reason for Ifá's appeal to honesty, orthopraxy, and humility.

Restoring the Connection

The world's religions and their Creation narratives usually point to a rupture of some sort at the time or immediately after the time of Creation. The Hebrew Scriptures tell the story of Eve's consumption of an apple as that rupture. The Kabbalah of the Jewish Mystical tradition offers a complex, technical description of a layered Creation of four worlds with a fifth near the seat of the Divine. This is the world of primordial man, Adam Kadmon—the spiritual prototype of the Adam of the Garden, near God's heart, yet unrealized in the Garden version.

The two Adams and God's fractured relationship with the physical representation of Adam, the primordial man, holds out Adam Kadmon as the exemplar of Divine intent. With OlOdù mare, divination provides the curative solution to the rupture. In traditional Judaism, the 613 mitzvot (commandments) perform similarly, restoring the Divine-human relationship.

The Commandments of Ifá work hand in hand with divination to build the type of human OlOdù mare intended to place on the earth—honest, humble, and just of action. Throughout life, the quest of Ifá's faithful is to become more just, humble, and honest, thus saving the original wound with obeisance to the work of the Creator God.

A restored connection between OlOdù mare and the people of Ifá is a restored Creation, healed by the loving connections of community and the connection of that community to a distant God. With the advice and learning provided by divination, the work of Ifá becomes an education for graceful, peaceful living. That process is one of healing shared between God and humanity.

One Creator God

OlOdù mare, despite the many names by which They are called, is only one God, situated as the source of all that is and the reason for all things, visible or invisible. In the next chapter, you will learn more about the Orisha, but they're often held up as evidence of a pantheistic model, which is not true of Ifá. Ifá is a monotheistic religion, just as Christianity, Judaism, and Islam are.

In the world of Ifá, all live in God's world and God, as all is within the context of the Supreme Being. There is no Church building. There is no hierarchy. There are roles fulfilled by people chosen to fulfill them, and the Orisha ordained by OlOdù mare to act as guides and helpers to humanity. Orunmila and Obatala are both Orisha, fulfilling specific roles, as directed by OlOdù mare. It is important to note that Orisha's spiritual beings were created by OlOdù mare, like everything and everyone else.

While it is futile to compare the roles of the Orisha, who are spiritual beings, to those of Angels or Saints, perhaps it's helpful to think of them as aspects of God, sent to work on behalf of the same distant Deity. This will be explored in more depth in Chapter Three, but it's helpful to have an idea as we talk more about divination from the perspective of God's relationship with humanity. It's important to understand that we are discussing a monotheistic Faith. To do that, we need to understand that the Orisha are not "gods" but rather facilitators of God and, like Obatala (High Priest) and Orunmila (Oracle), emissaries.

Another factor compelling some to depict Ifá as a polytheistic Faith is its sitting in Africa. It is not unusual for the West to mischaracterize African Faiths in this way. Colonialism brought with it the Christian Faith, and part of the colonialist project was to impose that Faith without compromise. There is also the matter of the many names of OlOdù mare.

This second reason for the polytheistic fallacy concerning Ifá is strange, as the God of the Hebrew Scriptures also has many names, from El-Shaddai to YHVH to Elohim. Thus, it is important to understand that this is a Western interpretation rooted in the usual human demand for priority in all things and a general lack of respect for practices and beliefs not native to them. That human demand is at the heart of the colonialist imposition of Christianity on populations who already had religious beliefs.

OlOdù mare is the most common name in Ifá for the Creator God, but regional variations have occurred with the diffusion of faiths to other regions and parts of the world. As we are discussing the traditional ways of Yoruba, here are the names OlOdù mare is known by in those communities of Faith:

- Oriki Edumare
- Oriki OlOdù mare
- Oriki Olorun

- Oriki Oluwa
- Oriki Odùmare

How we choose to name God is none of our business—as the narrative in the Book of Exodus discussed earlier so poignantly makes clear. The names of God exist to comfort the people by giving God a name that might be spoken in supplication. However, what is Divine can never be definitively named any more than it might be definitively known or described, despite humanity's most Herculean efforts.

The Attributes of Olodumare

The attributes of Olodumare are largely parallel to those of God in the three Monotheistic Faiths. As Creator, Olodumare is also all-knowing, all-powerful, the judge of all, without beginning or end, and the site of holiness.

Those attributes have uniqueness, reality, control, and complete, inviolable unity. Olodumare is reality itself in which all that exists resides, yet transcending the material and created. God, in this model, exists for Themselves in greatness as the immaterial First Cause, ultimate mystery, and eternality itself. From Olodumare flow fidelity, love, mercy, kindness, and all that is pure and good.

These attributes will sound familiar to practitioners of Islam, Christianity, and Judaism as the attributes of God described in their sacred books and practice. This familiarity brings us back to the journey of the Yoruba people to Nigeria.

From the Arabian Peninsula and its sacred cities, Mecca and Medina, the Yoruba cut across what is today known as the Middle East to arrive in Egypt. Who did they meet on that journey? Who did they absorb the cultural practices of? Who did they exchange their own cultural practices with?

The common threads running through Ifá, Judaism, Christianity, and Islam concerning the nature of God and the Creation narrative tell us a fascinating, ancient story. The bubbling cauldron of the ancient Near East contains myriad mysteries. The migratory trajectory of the Yoruba hints at some of them.

But when you are discussing an 8,000-year-old religion—senior to even the first of Near Eastern Monotheistic Faiths, Judaism—existing in a volatile, ancient world, the threads of history can become tangled. Any religion related to the ancient Near East is bound to have picked up and left behind various impressions and expressions as part of its journey through time and such religiously rich territories.

The Distant God Is Not Worshipped

Although Ifá is a monotheistic Faith, OlOdù mare is not expressly worshiped in Ifá. Rather, worship is directed to the emissaries of the distant God in the Orisha. Removed from humanity, OlOdù mare's presence is realized through the created spiritual beings representing Them and the ritual frameworks established for that purpose, especially divination.

The next chapter discusses Orisha and their counterparts, the Ajogun. Through the Orisha, humanity rediscovers its intended state. It returns to OlOdù mare's intention of creating it by communing with the Orisha through the agency of the Babalawo/Iyalawo.

Chapter 3: Emissaries and Stumbling Blocks

In the Ifá religion, as with its New World offshoots (Santeria, Voudon, et al.), Orisha stands as humanity's link to the Divine Reason at the center of the universe. Having moved out of range, OlOdù mare makes Their presence known through the Orisha, standing as representatives, emissaries, living links, and counselors interceding in human affairs on their behalf.

However, in the cosmology of Ifá, the world has a shadow side expressed in the presence of the Ajogun. While the Orisha are emissaries and helpers, the Ajogun are the stumbling blocks of the cosmos, leading humanity astray with ill intention.

Let us find out more about these two sides of Ifá's cosmological setup and what they mean in the context of religion, starting with the sunny side.

Mileage May Vary – The Orisha

Ifá lore insists that there are so many Orisha that they cannot be counted. At the same time, it is generally agreed that there are 400 of them, plus one. What this means is not that there are, in reality, 401 Orisha; it means that 400 plus one is an expression of limitless in the context of Ifá. The truth is that Orisha encompasses a wide variety of spiritual entities, including nature spirits who may be regionally appealed to but are otherwise unknown in the greater context of Ifá. Shortly, we shall talk about some of the Orisha known as the Seven African Powers, but it's important to remember that Ifá tradition itself numbers the Orisha variously. Depending on the specific community's oral tradition and source, it may be 400 or 1,400. The point is that the Orisha are numerous, and because they represent OlOdù mare, the mystery is entirely in order.

As pointed out, there is little illumination to be had in comparing the spiritual entities of Ifá with those of other faith systems. They are who they are, and the grace knows them through the religious system of which they form a vital part.

The most compelling description of the Orisha is that of emissaries of the Divine attributes and will. However, most of the Orisha were once like us—human beings. Having passed over to the spirit world, their destiny was to serve OlOdù mare as his emissaries and ordering agents. When you consider the immensity of such a commission and its Holy Source, it is a small wonder that there is no definitive number when it comes to the Orisha.

The Ajogun

Every cosmology needs balance. Without darkness, how is light distinguishable? Without evil, how is good known and defined? Ifá is no exception to this rule, with the balancing agent expressed as the Ajogun.

The problem of evil in Ifá is explained by the Eight Ajogun, who sow disease, discord, strife, misery, death, and chaos in human life. When they present themselves, the community's help to repel them is sought with the support of the learned Babalawo/Iyalawo.

We all know that everything in this world is not, by any means, good. The Judeo-Christian tradition explains this deficit in Creation with the fall of humanity in the Garden of Eden. In Ifá, evil in Creation is explained by these rogue spirits.

Unlike the Orisha, the Ajogun is not of human origin. They were never like us. Rather they express the negative aspects of the natural world and the adversity faced in every human life.

Before we meet some of these emissaries and stumbling blocks, let us talk about an unusual presence in the cosmology of Ifá—that of Eshu, the Divine Messenger and spirit of the crossroads.

OlOdù mare's Divine Messenger

One of Ifá's Orisha present at Creation, and thus, primordial, Eshu is the ordering agent mediating between life and death at the crossroads. Known for mischievousness, death, misfortune, and trickery, Eshu holds a special place in the cosmology of Ifá. Ensuring order and balance, Eshu is the communications director between humanity and OlOdù mare and the gatekeeper of communications with Orisha.

The Divine Messenger is also in charge of conveying sacrifices to the heavenly precincts to the Orisha they are intended for. But as Eshu is charged with balance, he also distributes sacrificial offerings to the Ajogun.

One of Eshu's primary traits is that he can go between good and evil. For this reason, he is sometimes cast as both Orisha and Ajogun. However, the truth is that he's neither, definitively. Eshu represents the continuing balance in Creation, dispensing the extremes of human existence according to his whim. He's as unpredictable as human life, reminding practitioners that "bad things happen to good people."

Because of this unpredictability, Eshu is known by more than 200 names, speaking to the diversity of action he's responsible for. Sometimes known as an "avenger" of wrongdoing, Eshu is also known to compel evildoing in humans for unknown purposes. Eshu presides over death and punishes the wicked, standing at the crossroads as God's gatekeeper and guiding the dead into life's next chapter.

Now that you have an idea of Ifá's cosmology, let us look at some of the major characters in that cosmology, starting with Orisha.

Major Orisha to Know

As this book is intended to introduce Ifá divination, it will limit it to the Seven African Powers. These are the principal Orisha of Ifá and are reasonably consistent in Ifá communities wherever they are found.

The Seven African Powers are also present in New World offshoots of Ifá, like Voudon, Candomble, and Santeria. These seven are the most powerful and evocative and, thus, the most widely revered of all the Orisha:

1. Orunmila
2. Obatala
3. Oshun

4. Ogun
5. Yemaya
6. Shango
7. Elegua

Of these seven, Shango is revered as the "king" of the Orisha, a powerful and fearsome Orisha charged with the stewardship and deployment of thunder. As with all that is concerned with unraveling the complexity of this ancient religion, the Seven African Powers may appear differently in different settings—for example, in Cuba, Babalu-Aye may be included in the place of one of the seven listed above.

There is some debate about the status of these seven Orisha, most of it centering on the presumed syncretism Ifá experienced under colonialism. But as with Santeria in Cuba, the Catholic Church was only appeased by Ifá practitioners. The Saints of the Church were superimposed, never obscuring the original identity of the Orisha masked by colonialism's wishful thinking. The Seven African Powers are not, as some suggest, Catholic Saints who are "not Orisha." Rather, they are Orisha who were hidden from the Church using its own iconography and thus preserved in their original, un-colonized form.

1. **Orunmila**

   In the Ifá Creation narrative, we met Orunmila, charged with being the link to OlOdù mare through divination. Through Orunmila, humanity is given the gift of spirituality and communication with the Divine and access to the Divine plan for their lives.

   Orunmila is the Orisha of wisdom and prophecy, moving among humanity as its spiritual advisor. He is also a co-creator, along with Obatala.

2. **Obatala**

   Again, we have met Obatala in the Creation story. Obatala acted as the "hands" of OlOdù mare in creating the universe. Obatala is the primordial Orisha, known in Ifá as humanity's co-creator and original sculptor. As you will recall, Obatala fashioned the human form, but OlOdù mare breathed life into it. The Yoruba say that he continues to form humans in the womb.

3. **Oshun**

   This female Orisha presides over Creation's rivers. She represents the font of Divine love, fertility, human love and romance, and the sweetness of life. She is both revered for her gentleness and feared for her temper. As mercurial and double-edged as water itself, Oshun's love can turn to rage when she is not respected.

4. Ogun

Presiding over metal and manipulating metals through alchemy, Ogun is believed to be made of iron himself. Ogun's sector is healing, but this Orisha is also sometimes compelled to destroy. Strength is Ogun's vibration, with a special place in his spiritual realm for families. Children, especially, are protected by Ogun.

5. Yemaya

Another female Orisha, Yemaya, is charged with water stewardship, like Oshun. But where Oshun's reign is over rivers, Yemaya's is over oceans. She protects women, children, and those who take to the ocean to fish and travel. Like Oshun and water itself, Yemaya can be unpredictable. However, she saves her tenderest care for abused women crying out for help and safety.

6. Shango

The Orisha of thunder, Shango, is intensely masculine. Dispensing justice with the lightning and thunder he commands, Shango is the archetypal male protector and hero. He is also virile, availing himself of female Orisha for his pleasure. He is revered as an ancient King of the Yoruba, becoming an Orisha after death. Once living as one of the most powerful leaders in human form, he's considered an Orisha of fearsome potency.

7. Elegua (Eshu)

Finally, we have Elegua (Eshu, the Divine Messenger). While unique among the Orisha and not strictly one of them (see OlOdù mare's Divine Messenger, earlier in this chapter), he stands as one of the Seven African Powers. Presiding over the crossroads where life and death converge, Elegua is a trickster and the official Guide to the Precincts of the Afterlife. This communications director allows humanity contact with the Orisha and, by extension, OlOdù mare.

Without Evil, What Is Goodness?

As with any other religious system, Ifá makes accommodation for the problem of evil. In the Hebrew Scriptures, the Book of Job dispatches this problem by explaining why bad things happen to good people.

Ifá's strategy concerning the problem of evil is not unlike that of modern ultra-Orthodox Judaism—devotion, prayer, and ritual. And as the Haredim of Judaism believe, the integration of religious belief into daily life is fundamental. The 613 mitzvot are a constant reminder of spiritual duty, and the Sixteen Commandments and 263 Odùs accomplish the same in Ifá.

Ifa's approach to good and evil quite similar to that of Judaism.
https://unsplash.com/photos/7a79GN3AZMM

Yoruba cosmology sees Creation as a gourd cut in half. Because of humanity's offensive behavior in the heavenly precincts, compelling OlOdù mare to move off the block, we live in one half alone. OlOdù mare and the Orisha (and ancestors) live in a far-removed "heavenly" half of Creation. Between these two halves reside the Ajogun and other evil spirits.

Without the orthopraxy (right action), ritual devotion, and prayerful worship of Ifá devotees, the Ajogun would wreak havoc, throwing Creation out of whack and creating chaos. As with the Haredim of Judaism, followers of Ifá believe that consecrating their daily lives to God keeps Creation from spinning out of control with the incursion of evil.

A constant in the cosmology of Ifá is death itself, framed as an inevitable part of human life and inseparable from it. For the Yoruba, death is inevitable, indivisible but not the end of anything.

Death is, in fact, a gateway to another chapter of life in the other half of the gourd. However, there are different values attached to death depending on when it arrives in the deceased person's life. For example, the elderly dying is greeted with jubilation. This is not because the old has died but because they have lived out their earthly quest for holiness. In the case of children or babies dying, the community reacts with sadness. That sadness has little to do with age, except in the reality that early death deprives the soul of life's journey toward holiness and sanctification. Death due to an accident or human interference (murder) is viewed similarly.

But the death of children is sometimes attributed to the principle of "abiku," in which children are reincarnated and never destined to reach adulthood. This is seen as a perpetual denial of the spirit's ascension and, thus, a curse. Abiku is translated as "spirit children" (children who have been denied the fullness of their spiritual potential).

The cosmology of Ifá recognizes no "final judgment." Rather, the lives we live stand as our testaments, typified by either vice or virtue. The community remembers us for what we have done in life, indicating the truth of our spiritual journeys on earth and our lessons. How we behave is how we proceed to the next chapter.

Without evil, there is no goodness. We cannot understand what is deemed "good" without the benchmark of evil providing a juxtaposition. And so, the cosmology of Ifá is intimately tied to the problem of evil and humanity's crucial role in containing it. With the Ajogun representing natural evil, a kind of contamination of Creation, the Divine OlOdù mare is separated from us. This immaterial wall of evil separates the two halves of the gourd. Ifá teaches worthy living, just action, and intense devotion to manage that wall's presence.

The next chapter explores the tools of Ifá. These are the physical components of divination as handed down at Creation and developed by the hands of humanity through the counsel of Orunmila. Let us see how the Babalawo/Iyalawo works with these tools to guide and counsel their communities and draw them forward on their spiritual journeys.

Chapter 4: The Tools of Ifá

This book explores an 8,000-year-old religion, Ifá, which is complex and not to be trifled with. If you are attracted to Ifá, we pray that your journey is blessed. However, even if that is the case, Ifá requires an intense initiation involving several stages and a complex set of ceremonies. Some of these ceremonies are private and secret to the practitioners of the religion. Even if you choose to be initiated into Ifá, you will not be using the tools described in this chapter. They are expressly reserved for the use of the Babalawo/Iyalawo, who has studied and trained for many years to ascend to the status of a learned spiritual teacher and guide.

In this era of instant gratification, our intention is not to proselytize but to inform, not to give license to dabblers but to share knowledge for the sake of interest. Thank you for respecting the practices of this ancient religion and its imperatives concerning membership and leadership.

The foundation of divination is the Odù—the verse that the Babalawo/Iyalawo is guided to by the casting done in divination. Divination leads to the revelation of the Odù as an answer to the supplicant's question, a solution to the challenge they are seeking divination to address.

The Babalawo/Iyalawo

The learned priest is the heart of Ifá, building on the communicative bridge represented by Orunmila, the spirit of wisdom. Orunmila, in turn, communicates all to OlOdù mare as the spiritual communications link between humanity and the Divine. The role of the priest is only attainable after a lengthy period of training and initiation—fifteen years by some accounts.

The priest is the "Father/Mother of Mysteries," divining the will of God in the lives of those he or she counsels. The "Ori" or "head" is the subject of the priest's work, which serves the individual destinies of community members and calls on them to apply intuition and intellect to life's challenges and questions.

Ori is the Divine spark in humanity. For this reason, it stands as an analog to the Orisha in the human body. Thus, while the Yoruba say that OlOdù mare has breathed life into them, the spark of that life is in the Divine attributes represented by the Orisha. Because of OlOdù mare's separation from humanity, the Divine spark's status is not directly Divine but mediated by Their attributes in Creation.

While Ifá priests are not necessarily selected for the vocation in childhood, children's spiritual gifts indicate "priest material." The prophetic role of the priest in divination is that of "clear sight," connecting the Ori of the person seeking counsel to Divine will and the power of the Orisha through the spirit of wisdom, Orunmila.

Orunmila may even be thought of as the first of all the priests. Having given human beings the gift of divination to ascertain the Divine will for their lives, he stands as the first in a long line of learned teachers, prophets, and counselors.

The role of the Babalawo/Iyalawo, while not limited to divination, is primarily that of a community resource, sharing the gift of Orunmila with the faithful. He is a shaman who seeks peace with all humanity, not just with the practitioners of Ifá. His commission is not only to those who share his beliefs but to humanity as a whole. A shaman, a traditional medicine man, and a healer of souls and bodies, the Babalawo/Iyalawo is the center of religious life in Ifá and the living link to the past, the future, and the heavenly realm of the spirits.

In divination, the Babalawo influences the status of problems or challenges in the lives of community members, calling on the intervention of Orunmila and other Orisha concerned with the person in question or the specific problem. The Babalawo has the power to influence outcomes by calling on this intervention, changing outcomes to those more favorable to the community member.

Women Priests — Tradition, Not Innovation

In most spiritual/religious traditions, women have been marginalized to the laity (those not ordained to serve the community). Despite indications in the scriptural record of religions like Christianity, where women fulfilled roles of ordained service in the earliest layer of the tradition, this is the universal truth.

Women played an important role as priestesses.
https://unsplash.com/photos/xZgkFQ4Hijc

For example, it was the "deaconess Phoebe" (Romans 1: 2) who bore the letter to the Romans—later to become a book in the Christian Scriptures—to the community in Rome. As she bore the letter, it would have been Phoebe who stood before that religious community to read its contents, written by Paul. While this latter function of the deaconess of the first century is assumed, the deacon's clerical role includes transmitting important information to the community from the bishop. Paul was not a bishop, as these did not exist at the time, but the modern deacon carries episcopal messages and delivers them to the parishes of any given diocese.

Primarily for reasons of social prohibition in Rome—women were relegated to a position lower than that of enslaved people)—women were marginalized out of leadership roles in the later Church, ceding these to men. It was not until the twentieth century that women began to regain their roles as leaders in sacramental worship and service to their communities.

However, the story of women's leadership in Ifá is very different. It is written right into the oral traditions of the religion, in the person of Orunmila's daughter. The story goes that Orunmila was asked why he was not initiating his daughter, Alara, into Ifá. He responded that she could not be because of her sex. He was corrected and advised that women had as much right to study Ifá as men. From then on, women were initiated into the priesthood.

IyanIfá and Iyalawo

While these two terms to describe women priests are used to define all women priests—especially online—there are some differences between the two.

"IyanIfá" is the more commonly used term, indicating stewardship of Ifá knowledge and the cultic empowerment required to engage in divination. "Iyalawo" is the more powerful of the two in terms of meaning.

"Iyalawo" indicates a person who has been graced with discernible spiritual gifts, traceable to the Creator God, OlOdù mare, through the wife of Orunmila, Odù—rumored by some branches of the Faith to have shared divination with Orunmila. Odù is considered the source of Aché (the spirit of humanity turned toward God and the life force). She is the primordial Iyalawo. In this last interpretation is the profound call to women in Ifá to take up the mantle of the priesthood.

Now, let us look at divination tools, what they are, how they're used, and their significance.

Opele — The Divining Chain

Viewed as the assistant of Orunmila, the divining chain echoes the form of the chain by which the Orisha (including Orunmila) traveled to the earthly realm from heaven. In its divining function, the Opele fulfills the same purpose figuratively, as a link between the two halves of Ifá's cosmological gourd.

Used primarily for minor divination work—daily concerns like money, sex, work, family, and romantic relationships or disputes between neighbors—the Opele is the most commonly used of all divination tools.

It is used by the Aseda and the Babalawo/Iyalawo, who might be likened to the deacon in the Christian clerical hierarchy, attending to the daily needs of the spiritual community, as opposed to the sacramental needs fulfilled by the priests.

The Opele consists of eight nuts of the Opele tree, divided in half and strung at equal intervals on a chain.

The chain is held at the center and swung gently. It is then laid out on a cloth in front of the priest. In a single motion, the priest creates a pattern, interpreted to correspond with an Odù (verse) of the oral tradition of Ifá, which is then recited.

Divination with Opele is part of a lifestyle in which the community is realigned with the Creator by taking their lives into their own hands by seeking the priest's counsel in divination. Ifá is considered primordial in the Faith and the general spiritual state of humanity as well. In the divination chain, practitioners find the solutions to their problems, solving them with the advice of Orunmila through the priest.

Ikin (Kola Nuts)

Ikin is nuts from the tropical Kola tree, called "Obi" or "Obi Abata" in the Yoruba language. The Obi Obata variety of Kola nut is sacred to Ifá. This type of nut from the Kola family consists of four lobes, which are the ones used in divination. The four-lobed Obi is also known as "Iya Obi" or "Mother Obi."

Kola Nuts.
Chinenye N., CC BY-SA 4.0 <https://creativecommons.org/licenses/by-sa/4.0>, via Wikimedia Commons https://commons.wikimedia.org/wiki/File:Red_and_yellow_kola_nuts.jpg

The four-lobed Obi is used in divination due to the perception of balance between male and female energies, with two lobes representing the male sex and two the female sex. The number four represents stability and consistency inherent in the balance of energies.

Only when the Obi is split open are the four lobes revealed. They are distinguishable as male or female by the markings that appear down the center of the lobe. A single line terminating in a point indicates the sex for the male. For the female, the line splits in two, resulting in the shape of a "y."

The metaphysics of the Ifá religion specifies that all energies are divisible into male and female, but the distinction is not only concerned with the specificities of sex. The male/female dichotomy of energetic reality in Ifá provides a benchmark for understanding energy as a spiritual simulation of dichotomous mammalian sex.

All the usual attributes associated with the two sexes are present in the energetic interpretations of Ifá, without assigning them a value according to the sex they describe. While male energy is routinely typified as expansive and open, female energy is described as circumscribed and closed; this religion does not attach these qualities to the sex in question, nor does it attach any value judgments to energies deemed "negative" or "positive." The energies indicated just "are," without ascribing any value rooted like the sex itself. Energy is just energy in Ifá.

Interpreting the Lobes

Iya Obi divination starts with the lobes and the way they land on the divination tray (which is discussed next). Instrumental in interpretation are the markings on the lobe and the way they land. When the marking is visible after the lobe lands, it is read as "open." When not visible, it's interpreted as "closed." In the basic level of Iya Obi divination, the way the Iya Obi lobe falls is the whole story. In the more sophisticated levels of divination, the "sex" of the lobe comes into play, adding another layer of interpretation. At this level of divination, open sections are recorded as "O" and closed sections as "X."

Kola nuts are selected for divination when they are four-lobed but also at their freshest. When the nut has been around for a while, it can begin to crack, rendering the internal lobes visible. This nut cannot be used in divination.

The divination tray is used with the Iya Obi. Traditionally made of wood, the tray is elaborately carved by artisans dedicated to producing the sacred article. The intricate carvings are intended to honor the work of the priest.

The tray calls out to the Divine Messenger Elegua/Eshu to facilitate communication with Orunmila and through Orunmila, the other Orisha. The tray is covered with a white powder called "Iyerosun" (divining powder). This powder is produced by termites feasting on the Iyerosun tree. Without using this powder to the Opon Ifá, divination with the Opon Ifá cannot occur. Iyerosun is an integral component of the divination system of Ifá.

Opon Ifá, Spread with Iyerosun

Like the Opele, the Opon Ifá is used to discover the Odù (verse or story), indicated by the position of the Kola nut lobes when they fall and the movement of the Iyerosun dust resulting from the casting of the lobes.

Carvings around the perimeter of the Opon Ifá are more than just decorative. They indicate nine distinct sections to further support the interpretation of the Iya Obi and Iyerosun. Each of these sections represents the person of a revered ancient diviner.

The priest's job is to determine the Odù indicated by throwing nut lobes. The 256 Odù all have a place in divination, determined by the casting and marks made in the Iyerosun. The Odù indicated also determines the nature of the offerings to be applied to the problem the session addresses. The Odù is also associated with individual spirits and situations. Just as there are only a limited number of plot lines based on common human themes and problems, there are prototypical life challenges indicated by the Odù and sought in divination.

As mentioned earlier, the Opele is sometimes used in divination with the Opon Ifá. Opele is usually employed to discern the forward conduct of minor matters. Weightier problems and challenges are addressed by using the Iya Obi ikin.

A Blueprint for Living

The purpose of divination is the eventual perfection and purification of the human soul, refined in the practical and often challenging context of human life. Divination, the gift of OlOdù mare through the Oracle, Orunmila, is a link to Divine direction through the Orisha. Calling on the practice for guidance and self-reflection as a life discipline provides valuable information to better human life.

However, of all the characteristics of Ifá divination, perhaps the most genuinely surprising is guidance that is capable of changing the course of one's life. The Yoruba do not believe that the average human life is buffeted by the capricious winds of the universe—with notable exceptions like "spirit children," locked in a cycle of eternal immaturity. Instead, they believe that the individual is empowered to change the course of their life, taking charge by taking ownership.

This may sound suspiciously like the postmodernism assertion that we can create reality, but Ifá's philosophical framework and cosmology present the idea of self-empowerment differently. Divination answers human questions with the limitless experience of the Orisha, God's emissaries. Divination searches for the Odù that fits, and the questioning person seeks counsel and the answers sought. Yet those answers must be carried forward into life to represent genuine and profound change.

In Ifá, change is not optional when required. Change is the responsibility of the individual practitioner because what the individual does ripples outward, impacting the community's coherence and cohesion. Just as a pebble dropped in a puddle displaces and changes the water, so does the person resisting change. There is no excuse in Ifá for a refusal to follow the counsel of the learned Babalowa/Iyalawo, acting as a conduit to the spirit world. There is a commandment about that, if you recall.

While postmodernism counsels change for the benefit of the individual alone with no accommodation to anyone or anything, Ifá counsels change for the benefit of the individual in a material and spiritual community. In the material community, only goodness and decency retain the strength of the fabric. In the spiritual community of the Orisha and ancestors, the same is true. Individual action and challenges impact both halves of the cosmic gourd with equal force.

The divination work is much larger than any priest or community member seeking guidance and life improvement. It is bigger than discerning the way forward of the community in leadership or seeking the will of the Divine in matters of conflict and disharmony. The work of Orunmila's divinely inspired gift was of union between the two halves of the gourd, once separated by misbehavior, rudeness, and disregard for the dignity of the sacred.

Throughout life, Ifá practitioners build themselves into someone who is eventually remembered with affection and respect and welcomed by the world of spirits. Divination is the tool that draws this blueprint for living, spiritualizing the material and materializing the spiritual. Divination is the healing of Creation and the healing of human souls.

Chapter Five will discuss the casting of the ikin. You will find out how the Opon Ifá and the Iyerosun interpret the resulting configurations to arrive at the right Odù for the subject of the divination session.

Again, as a reminder, casting the ikin is not for the uninitiated (those who are not members of Ifá). Even those so initiated should also be initiated into the priesthood of the Babalawo/Iyalawo to practice divination. Please respect this ancient religion's tenets and prohibitions while enjoying your journey of discovery.

Chapter 5: How Ifá Is Cast and an Introduction to Odù Ifá

"Yoruba ethics: To become, through ritual, a being who knows more and understands more, a person who lives more and is more."

Ulli Beier

Something important to understand about divination and the interpretation of the ikin and Iyerosun is the Odù itself and what accompanies it. Many complex calculations must be made according to the casting signs on the Opon Ifá. These determine not only the Odù but also the gifts and sacrifices required to accomplish the effect or favor being sought.

Casting the kola nut lobes is a complicated, formulaic enterprise, demanding an impressive command of the used tools. There are many moving parts involved, and one of those moving parts is the Odù (which is discussed later)—the verse indicated by the casting. The application of the Odù to the problem being presented often helps the questioner connect the dots involved. The intervention of the Orisha through the Babalawo/Iyalawo and Eshu, the Divine Messenger, is mediated by the human priest. The priest reads, considers, and produces the Odù that has been spoken to him on the Opon Ifá.

This is not a "psychic reading." Ifá divination is a complex system of signs, prayer, praise, intention, ritual, and interpretation, requiring a sensitive diviner and a receptive supplicant, both focused on acquiring information that will move the individual—and thus the community—forward in spirit.

Preparing the Opon Ifá and Ikin

The priest and supplicant will be seated on the floor, and the Opon Ifá will sit before the Babalawo, with the "foot" of the tray nearest to him. The priest will be facing east. A tool used only in ikin/Opon Ifá divination, the iroke Ifá will be at the priest's side. This tapper will be used to summon Eshu and Orunmila by tapping it on the side of the Opon Ifá. This also calls forth the nine ancient revered diviners depicted around the edges of the Opon Ifá. The tray will have been spread with Iyerosun. This powder will be divided into nine sections corresponding to the nine great diviners. The Babalawo/Iyalawo will praise these revered ancestors.

Using the right hand, the ikin lobes will start to be packed in the priest's left hand. As there are sixteen in total, and they can be quite large, the kola nuts will begin to fall. When only one or two lobes are in the left hand, the priest is ready to cast. If more than two lobes remain, the packing process must be repeated until only one or two kola nut lobes remain.

Casting

The lobes are cast when only one or two kola nuts remain in the Babalawo/Iyalawo's hand. If one remains, the Iyerosun will be marked with two vertical strokes. If two, the powder will be inscribed with two vertical strokes.

This process is repeated eight times, resulting in various configurations that mean different things, directing the priest toward the appropriate Odù. This is determined by the markings made on the Opon Ifá, revealing the nature of the Odù. However, the supplicant's reason for seeking a divination session also figures in the priest's discernment.

When the left side of the Opon Ifá's markings matches those on the right side of the tray, the Odù is revealed. But these markings all refer to specific Odù, appearing in specific parts of the corpus of Ifá.

Names and symbols correspond to every Odù, with single lines denoting the "light" or open position and the double lines representing the "dark" or closed position (as discussed in the section on ikin in Chapter Four). However, there are two sets of signs produced in ikin casting.

The second set of symbols consists of the binary "0" and "1," with the 0 representing the "dark" or closed position and the 1 representing the "light" or open position. These are known as the "meji" Odù. This second set of signs is used only when the opele (divination chain) is used to cast.

The interpretation and process of casting may seem simple enough on the surface. But it is a complex matter that requires many years of training. As part of their initiation, priests must memorize the Odù Ifá.

With its 256 Odùs, this collection of spiritual knowledge expands and grows constantly. There is no canonization process, and, over time, some of the information contained in the Odù Ifá has been lost. However, revelation to the people is a continual thing. It does not stop when a hierarchical organization decides it should because the conversation between Olodumare and humanity is ongoing and eternal.

Within each of the 256 Odù are "ese," and there may be as many as 800 of these in every Odù. In the ese, the ongoing conversation is most vibrant, as these are added constantly to reflect new knowledge. For that reason, there is no accurate accounting of how many there are. Thus, imagine that the priest must commit all this information to memory to be prepared to provide supplicants with an accurate divination session. (See Resources for a link to a table with the symbols for every Odù in the Odù Ifá.)

Next, you will explore the Odù Ifá, what it means, and its role in Ifá divination.

The Odù Ifá

The understanding of Ifá is rooted in the Odù Ifá, a collection of parables and instructions that set out guidelines for ethical living. It is said that the Odù Ifá is a collection of binary codes (see the second set of symbols above, which are quite literally "0"s and "1"s). These codes express the totality of universal energy, coursing through the two halves of Ifá's cosmic gourd.

This energy gives life to all that lives, and within it resides every permutation of human life and its challenges. Fortune and misfortune, blessing and curse, birth and death, and everything in between are found in this book of ethical, moral, and spiritual wisdom.

The sixteen major Odù (Meji/Oju Odù) are first. The other 240 Odù are elaborations and commentary on the first sixteen. In the Odù are the keys to living well and the healthy spirituality that accompanies a well-lived life. The Odù are oracles in and of themselves.

Each Odù contains detailed information about solving the problems and challenges of life, with instructions as to how the supplicant is to approach the solution, including the attendant rituals, medicinal responses, and sacrifices required to affect a fitting response that pleases the Orisha.

In the ese contained in the Odù are poetic instructions directing followers to their obligations to the Orisha and the best course of action to resolve the problem or question brought to divination.

The Odù Ifá is not a codified (written) tradition. It is a large corpus of oral tradition, passed down from priest to priest and committed to memory. Any written expressions you see are secondary to the pure tradition of Ifá. And while there is an "app for that"—yes, a phone app—it is clear that such innovations are not in the spirit of this ancient religion.

The Blueprint behind the Blueprint

Odù Ifá, with its binary codes and energetic basis, serves as a blueprint for divination. While divination offers a blueprint itself, that blueprint evolves over time, with the Odù Ifá as its true foundation. Without the knowledge presented by the corpus of Yoruban wisdom, there is no point in divination. And without the Babalawo/Iyalawo, there is no knowledge. Without these two elements reaching out to the Orisha on behalf of the supplicant, there is no divination. It has no meaning.

Divination is a gateway to the knowledge through the spirit that Ifá is rooted in. As cornerstones of the faith, intelligence and wisdom are developed through the gift of divination, teaching, and admonishing the supplicant to know more and live more fully (see the quote at the start of this chapter). Intelligence and wisdom, supported by the Odù Ifá and its teachings and prescriptions, are the way to "Ori," the soul's destiny and path in life and death; the seat of intellect, wisdom, and spirituality. As the "head," the Ori stands in a similar position to the concept of free will in the Christian religion.

The spark of consciousness alive in the human being is the ability and the power to change the self to more closely resemble the Divine primordial vision. And in the Ori is the spiritual consciousness, working in concert with the intellect. When the Ori encounters Odù Ifá in divination, it is dignified and expanded, becoming the Orisha it is intended to be. The Ori is the "divine self," beyond the mere mortal human organism's presumed default settings. In fact, the Ori is an emanation of the Divine, giving it the status of a personal Orisha.

Orthopraxy

In the Ifá religion, orthopraxy is not just built into daily life in the Sixteen Commandments. It is implied by divination itself. When you ask someone for advice in a religious setting, and they go to great lengths to give it to you, ignoring that advice is an act of profound disrespect. And to insult or disrespect the Babalawo/Iyalawo is to break the Sixteenth Commandment (see Chapter One).

Orthopraxy, the "right action" that typifies the ideal Ifá life on earth, is played out in the very structure of the religion, guiding the practitioner closer to a spiritual ideal that serves both halves of the Divine gourd, bringing harmony in the actions of those who are learning to live well. Without reflection, there is no action, so orthopraxy is an action arising from and guided by reflection.

It might be said that orthopraxy has its foundation in wisdom. Having grown from the integration of thought and emotion in Ori, wisdom seeks the good in all things, practicing what it preaches by acting following what is right and good. These actions lead to the harmonious conduct of life by the individual in the surrounding community.

Moreover, in Ifá, the community is a microcosm of Creation itself, modeling the attributes of Olodumare, as expressed in the Orisha. All are brought together in orthopraxy when the talk becomes the walk.

In the Ifá religion, talk is constructive, not demonstrative. To talk is to explore solutions, instructions, and prescriptions. It is to share tradition toward the betterment of human life. It's not to sing of one's devotion. When the right action is the imperative of the community, talk is cheap. The action does all the talking, reifying belief as just behavior that gives more than it takes.

The Ancestors Speak

Collected in the corpus of the Odù Ifá is the wisdom of generation upon generation of Ifá believers. Refining and enhancing through time with new knowledge and insights, the living, growing nature of these verses is probably what is most extraordinary.

This oral tradition is vast, encompassing knowledge gathered over 8,000 years. This knowledge is assembled to guide practitioners with tools that have survived time to come to them as gifts of wisdom. Primarily, these are etiological (an explanation of why things are the way they are) and expository (explanations about how things happen and how to deal with them) narratives. Within those narratives are the archetypes represented by the Odù themselves, symbolizing the vast, untapped knowledge in the collective unconscious of humanity.

As we move forward in subsequent chapters to read more about the Odù Ifá, the simplicity and ethical soundness of its contents will become apparent. The Odù Ifá is the great blueprint of a life driven by the seeking after wisdom through the agency of the intellect. The priest can only share what has been divined. The diviner can only tell the supplicant what has been indicated on the Opon Ifá by the ikin or the opele.

Once the divination session has been accomplished, it is the supplicant's responsibility to act; to perform the orthopraxis demanded by the verses indicated, the urgings of the Orisha, and the work of the Babalawo/Iyalawo.

When the ancestors and Orisha speak through divination, the wisdom of experience accumulated over 8,000 years is laid out to the living. And that experience guides right action, helping the living live more authentically and less anxiously. The ultimate truth is that humanity is not created for its own sake but to bring harmony to a troubled Creation.

Chapter 6: Odù Ifá I, Part One — Ogbe and Oyeku

The remainder of this book focuses on the Odù Ifá, with each of the final seven chapters representing the four distinct sections of these teachings, with each section divided into two chapters for the sake of readability, save the last one, which is less complex.

Before we begin, it is helpful to think of the Odù as archetypes (in the Jungian sense). As you read about each chapter's function and its place in the lives of the Ifá faithful, know that the Ifá concept of consciousness is very similar to that proposed by Carl Jung. The Odù represent various energetic realities in the universe connected to consciousness. Like Jung's archetypes, the Odù are models existing in the collective unconscious, which are incomprehensible to us until the time we can absorb their message comes. The Odù are the energies that must be learned to understand one's destiny and humanity's collective destiny.

This chapter will cover the four sections noted above, starting with Ogbe (also referred to as Ejiogbe Oguna or Ogbe). Ogbe's teachings about Ori concern the practitioner's ability to heed the promptings of the intellect in spirit, guiding them in the right direction. When you can unquestioningly listen to these promptings, you are trusting what is known to most of us as "intuition."

The Ori, the seat of our destiny and intuitive sensing capacity, is the most important of all our faculties in the Ifá worldview. This is where answers may be sought and found, so Ogbe directly instructs Ifá adherents on how they might use what they have learned to heed Ori and trust it implicitly.

Ori — The Hidden Orisha

The Ori, that personal core where thought and emotion are processed to help us make decisions and make sense of life, is the divine kernel of the human being. In it, we see the tremendous potential of human intelligence. For this reason, it is an Orisha unto itself, defining our consciousness and its movement through the world.

This tells us that the divine kernel in the human being is the way toward our fullest potential. In Christianity, the soul is somewhat analogous to the idea of Ori but is not of the same stature. In Christianity, the soul is subject to God. In Ifá, the Ori acts as Divine Will filtered through the human intellect and spirit, becoming its own reflection of Divine Nature. However, the Ori is unique to the human animal. We are precious in the sight of the Divine and worthy to carry such an encouraging truth as the Ori within us. But the Ori is to be developed. It is deposited as a vessel of our efforts. Like the Christian concept of salvation, it is freely given but sanctified by the recipient's efforts of such a tremendous gift.

Yet, that does not mean Ori is born autonomous. It's trained to be so. It's a life's work to leverage the fullness of the Ori's capacity for orthopraxy and train the mind to understand what that is in any given situation. The Ori is a vessel of wisdom, guided by the work of divination, which leads the practitioner to the Odù Ifá and its multitudinous lessons for leading a life worthy of Olodumare's goodness.

Leadership 101

The teachings of Ogbe encompass the qualities humans tend to expect in a leader, counseling that we all have these qualities in an undeveloped form. While some people may model leadership naturally, that describes few people. Most of us need to learn what leadership looks like by encountering good examples of it.

Thus, with the priest as a guide, the practitioner attends to the Ori as a means of finding within it the qualities of leadership. Modeled by Olodumare, the priest, and the Orisha, the Ifá practitioner, is guided toward her capacity to model the qualities demanded of leaders to benefit family, community, and Creation itself.

The qualities of a leader, as interpreted by Ogbe, may be readily found in the Sixteen Commandments of Ifá, a thumbnail of the teachings of Odù Ifá. These sixteen basic teachings all encourage honesty, integrity, decency, humility, compassion, and empathy. The ideal leader has all these qualities and more to spare, so self-development becomes a goal to be the best version of yourself possible.

Patience Is the Start of Good Character

Take a quick look around, and you will see that most people are impatient and emotionally dysregulated. We act before we think. We throw tantrums when we do not get what we want, and our drive for instant gratification is constantly fed in a society driven by technological immediacy.

However, patience is the mark of someone who has learned that the alternative does not get you very far. When we are impatient, we say things we don't mean. We allow our emotions to get the better of us because we don't know how to control them. This leads to extreme social volatility, which is neither desirable nor necessary. The ability to control our emotions in the presence of triggers and stressors is one factor that keeps us from going off and suffering the consequences that follow. Without patience, we're like babies waking up from an afternoon nap, screaming over trivial matters like a slow barista or a late bus. When we have the patience required to wait for things to work out as they eventually will, we're in control of our emotions instead of allowing them to control us.

Temperance in All Things

The human temperament is an unruly beast, so Ifá rightly sets out to tame it, and it does so not with prohibitions but with prescriptions. While many of the Sixteen Commandments of Ifá have a distinct "don't" orientation, the net effect suggested by following them is entirely positive. And the work of Ogbe is similarly positive.

Temperance is an important factor in Ifa.
https://unsplash.com/photos/OptEsFuZwoQ

Temperance has more than health benefits for the human organism. It has a mediating effect on emotions by helping to maintain balance. When out of balance, we are out of sorts, out of patience, and into a whole new size of clothes! That is the problem with instant gratification. Patience demands that we wait to be gratified. It further demands that we still our impatience to wait for the best possible outcome. That outcome only arrives when we sit on the fidgeting toddler within.

The Self-Indulgence of Negativity

While we are living in an undoubtedly self-indulgent age, it is clear that many of us have always been that way. Humans tend to have a belief in the uniqueness of their experiences. We cling to this belief so passionately that we cannot imagine any other destiny than the one we have convinced ourselves is our birthright.

We have all had gifts and vocations, but even if this is the case, they are wasted when the will to employ them fruitfully is not present. We throw out the champagne, uncorked. There is brilliance in every Ori in every human being, but the self-indulgence of negativity can easily squash that brilliance.

Negativity is a type of egotism that demands that destiny conforms to worldly imperatives. However, the Ori is not mocked. Choosing not to listen to the Ori is, in Ifá, choosing to ignore the voices of the ancestors through the Babalawo/Iyalawo. It chooses the unreal over the real, the world over the spirit.

And in this choice is a return to the original division of the great gourd of the cosmos. We were cavalier. God was not amused, so Olodumare withdrew, putting a little distance between the Divine and material Creation. The rejection of the wisdom available to people in the Ifá tradition, for whatever reason, creates a small rupture in the relationship with Olodumare and the spirit world and, thus, with the ancestors. That is profoundly negative, affecting the community in its very fabric.

Even when born with an undeniably stellar destiny, there are people in this world who choose to wander aimlessly, looking for themselves in an external narrative. Yet, the true destiny of the individual is alive in the Ori, and when it is fed and fostered, acknowledged, and heeded, the Ifá follower grows to the Ori's full stature.

True leadership is not being a figurehead or a "top dog." True leadership is being a light among others and leading the way by deed and word. Our thoughts and emotions are integrated into Ori in growing wisdom; we are equipped to deploy our words and deeds to the good. When that is done consistently, we're leaders, lighting the way for others.

Obatala's Legacy

Obatala is described in the oriki (praise poetry) dedicated to him:

> *"He is patient.*
> *He is silent.*
> *Without anger, he pronounces his judgment."*

And the virtue of patience toward just judgment, meditating on the factors involved, and dispensing deliberative justice, is how he is depicted. In this respect, the Ogbe of Odù Ifá stands as a description of the attributes of the co-creating Orisha—Olodumare's right-hand man, if you will. However, the oracle, Orunmila, is of a similar deliberative, patient temperament.

One of Ogbe's illustrative ese's tells of Orunmila's extraordinary patience. The Orisha is said to wait three years if offended. This, explains Orunmila, allows the transgressor to correct the offense given. Even when given to pass judgment, the oracular Orisha moves deliberately, measuring his steps not in time but awareness.

The fact that these two Orisha are so central to this chapter of Odù Ifá makes clear that the practitioner is being trained to contain visceral emotional responses after the example of two of the most prominent primordial Orisha. Neither acts precipitously, choosing slow, deliberate action that leads (logically) to well-founded decisions. Many wars might be avoided with such a robust moral framework in play.

The message of Ogbe is that the development of patience and emotional regulation is the foundation of Ori's true realization. When we have control of ourselves, we have control of the world around us, reacting with measured, thoughtful action. Leadership relies on such action and such a process of patient deliberation to pursue justice and orthopraxy.

The Objective of Patience

The Ogbe states:

> *"Nothing of any value is created by an uncontrolled temper.*
> *Patience is the foundation of existence.*
> *A patient person has the world.*
> *She will grow old in bliss.*
> *His health will be robust.*
> *She will live a life of happiness and enjoyment,*
> *With the taste of honey on her tongue."*

As with most of the proscriptions and prescriptions we read in Chapter One's review of the Sixteen Commandments, the reward of good is in doing good, and the reward of patience is in the ripe fruit it bears.

Reaching up to pluck an apple from a tree that has not ripened is no victory. It cannot be eaten with pleasure. But the wise person whom Ori counsels that the apple must be left to ripen eats with pleasure when the fruit is ready to be enjoyed in its full delight.

The fruit of patience is the same—patience blooms with time and practice. We learn to contain our reactions. We learn to examine the moment with clear eyes, seeing all around us. We learn to be human in a way that honors the gift of being born to this legacy of our Ori's guidance through the world.

Patience is at the heart of emotional regulation. When we learn to examine our emotions, assigning them the value they deserve and nurturing them as part of us, we acknowledge them. At the same time, we put them in their place, knowing they can be dangerous influences when left unexamined. With our emotions in our command by virtue of our intellect, we can more readily step out into the world in the confidence that we're not going to lose it today, that we're going to be aware, informed humans. We walk in the confidence of the evolved self when we command our emotions and understand our thoughts.

Leadership is in the living of its role among human communities—the modeling of a way to live together in harmony, free of rancor and unnecessary competition. It is how we treat others, never leading astray or saying what we know not to be true. These simple rules for living are the social connective tissue that binds us together in love, leading one another to a less stressful way of living together.

In that binding is the reconstruction of our relationship with Olodmare.

Oyeku

Oyeku is the very heart of the darkness of the void—that which we do not know but will someday. It is the beginning and the end of all things.

Oyeku means death, but it means so much more. Oyeku is the unknown eternality of things. We are unconscious of it unless we are philosophers or students of religion. However, even such people cannot hope to penetrate the fullness of the mystery that is Oyeku. That is for the spirit world and those who inhabit it.

In Oyeku is the journey of life, unfolding eternally and simultaneously, in a place with no time, no space as we know it, no materiality, and no passions. Time has one meaning here—the cycles of life just turn. Those cycles are many in our lives, made cycle after cycle. Those cycles teach us how to prepare the soul for the greatest adventure of all: Death.

The Circle Is Unbroken

To seek commonalities in the philosophical underpinnings of the world's religions is not to seek integration or syncretization; rather, it is to understand how deeply ingrained in human thinking the circular model of time is.

We live in a circular, cyclically bound cultural setting, wherever we are. Assumptions are made about how we shall live depending on age, sex, attractiveness, and intellectual ability. In almost every society, birth is followed by some form of education, then marriage, then offspring. These milestones represent cycles that we are compelled to realize—whether they are appropriate for us or not—because there was a period before the recorded time when our survival depended on the realization of these milestones.

Reflecting on the concept of Oyeku frees the intellect to apprehend destiny as part of that dark reality. In Oyeku is an unknown that may be known. But not now. To truly be in the unbroken circle of life, we must be awake to all of it, including the inevitability of death.

To the Ifá, death is not the unknown but part of the life we know. Thus, death continues this life, taking with us all we have learned in our spiritual journeys to the spirit world, just as the ancestors did before us. In Ifá, it is thought that only the ignorant fear death. The learned and integrated person, connected to their Ori, does not fear death but approaches it mindfully. They step carefully toward that horizon that never arrives, aware, awake, and ready for the next chapter and the chapter after that.

To be ready for death—no matter when it comes—is to be ready to know Oyeku, this womb of nothingness and progenitor of life's cycles. Without fear, the Ifá respectfully and consciously approach her hallowed precincts. All things begin, and all things end. These realities are part of living a conscious, dignified, and satisfying life. Both beginnings and endings are good because nothing ever truly ends.

This chapter has covered some key concepts and features of Ifá that will help you contextualize the content of subsequent chapters, giving you a brief grounding of Ifá's core ideas and how they are presented in the Odù Ifá.

The four sections of the Odùe Ifá covered in this part of the book have been broken into two chapters each. The next chapter covers the next two Odù s of Odù Ifá I.

Chapter 7: Odù Ifá I, Part Two — Iwori and Odi

This chapter will explore Part Two of Odù Ifá I in the Odù s of Iwori and Odi and their energetic roles in the teachings imparted by divination.

Iwori

Iwori is another tremendously profound metaphysical concept that has to do with consciousness. In Ifá, everything that exists has a type of consciousness. It may not be like human consciousness, but it is consciousness nonetheless.

Iwori is a penetrating gaze, discerning consciousness as an entity unique to the bearer, seeing the process of consciousness itself as one of individualization. In practice, Iwori is transformation, a feat accomplished by applying fire. In the case of Iwori, that fire is passion.

Passion has many faces. They are not all pretty. Passion can lead to the birth of children, sanctified partnerships, and the accomplishment of great change. However, passion can also lead to conflict, even the extreme war conflict. Thus, to understand Iwori, we should understand transformation as being wrought in the fire of passion, but the passion generating the fire is mindful. This is not the unbridled passion that passes after the heat of the moment has subsided. Transformation is sustained fire. The fire of passion, like the material fire in which gold may not be eliminated but only refined, reveals the purity of the soul.

Individualization and Consciousness

Ori is the key to arriving at an understanding of Iwori. The Ori, as discussed in the last chapter, is both consciousness and the destiny of that consciousness. It is the seat of the soul and our self-concept. With divination, Ori is tried as a precious metal—by the fire of passion that leads to transformation.

It is Iwori that most directly confronts Ori. Through its penetrating gaze, Iwori reaches toward the Ori with the fire it needs to be transformed. This is the Divine gaze that knows us and is part of us simultaneously, with the Ori as its throne in the human body. Iwori links our consciousness/destiny and the spirit world and the Divine.

The individualized unit of consciousness is, of course, the human being. We are this consciousness, enfleshed because we perceive ourselves. We are self-conscious and aware that we are we. I am me. You are you. We know ourselves as units of consciousness, moving through the world in the borderland of flesh that defines us as the human organism, making us intelligible to those we encounter in the world.

Our flesh, acted upon by our consciousness, is how we know the world around us. We touch, taste, smell, hear, and see the world in our senses. In our consciousness, we interpret the senses as received. However, it is all one thing, working as a single unit of consciousness. The flesh communicates to the consciousness the sensation, flavor, scent, sound, and sight we experience, revealing it as information to be interpreted.

For Ifá, this is all learning, feeding the Ori. That feeding is accompanied by the gift of divination, further feeding the Ori. The fire is born in the interaction of the individual with the truths of life revealed to him in Odù Ifá. The supplicant is given a choice in divination—to be alive to the guidance of the Orisha or to shrink from it. Yet, as discussed, it is not really a choice at all when you think of what is to be gained by building on the lessons of divination translated to orthopraxy.

The Fire of Transformation

Iwori, that penetrating gaze, brings the fire to the soul by any number of means. Learning is chief among them, but sometimes, people need to feel the fire before learning. That can be transforming, too. Adversity is often transformative. Sometimes bad things happen to good people, especially in Ifá, so they can learn something important.

Because of our individualized consciousness, human beings experience the world in myriad ways. What is fascinating for one is tedious for another. What brings happiness to you brings misery to someone else. This person-to-person individualization of consciousness is leveraged in Ifá to speak directly to the Ori. The uniqueness of the Ori in each person is the proving ground of a life lived mindfully, spiritually, and in community with other, individualized units of consciousness.

Look around and ask yourself what is at the heart of most Western societal problems. For some, it is the elevation of the individual above all considerations. What the individual chooses to do has more weight than what the community needs the individual to do. We can see this most clearly in resistance to the COVID vaccine.

The individualized consciousness, aware of itself and other units of consciousness, is potential. In Ifá, that potential is to be deployed toward the cohesion of the community, rooted in tradition, guided by divination and the Odù Ifá. It is not expressly for itself. Rather, it recognizes that the whole is greater than a component thereof.

A Conscious Universe?

As stated earlier, the Ifá viewpoint is that everything in Creation has consciousness. But what if the universe itself was conscious? Emerging research is asking that very question.

Ifa questions the consciousness of the universe.
https://unsplash.com/photos/oMpAz-DN-9I

Materialism has been the predominant scientific explanation for consciousness—that consciousness emanates from activity in the brain.

The Platonic/Cartesian mind-body split is favored—consciousness is separate from the body, existing independently as the "soul." Now, enter panpsychism, which posits a consciousness inhabiting every fiber of the universe.

As it observes what is around us, our individualized consciousness is separate yet contained in this universal consciousness, giving awareness to every material thing. Biological organisms—including us—continually make decisions rooted in consciousness without even thinking about it. When confronted with a stairway, we climb. When confronted with a wall, we find a way to get around it. We change our behavior to accommodate what we have encountered in the world. These automated decisions concerning physical navigation are consciousness, too.

Moreover, while panpsychism continues to be a marginal theory of consciousness, the idea of consciousness found "out there, somewhere" and "everywhere there is" points to Iwori. The penetrating gaze of consciousness outside ourselves, observing and interacting with our individualized consciousness, may sound like science fiction. However, in the world of discerning humanity's relationship to spirit, Iwori as a function of universal consciousness seems plausible. While speculative, panpsychism changes the channel of our understanding of consciousness, which does not seem to be able to formulate a definitive response about what it is.

Perhaps consciousness—the universal kind, external to our units of consciousness—is the penetrating gaze of Iwori, inviting us to transform. In that gaze is the fire of passion, urging humanity toward a spirituality that is equally penetrating, binding all consciousness together in a singular purpose.

Ministering to the Ori, Iwori's gaze is laser-focused, producing the spark that will provoke the conflagration that burns away all that is unworthy, liberating it to proceed toward its destiny in awareness. Awareness, then, is the gift that is transformed because if the universe is consciousness, we are its spiritual messengers through the Divine Ori.

Our thoughts and emotions integrated, we are transformed under the penetrating gaze of Iwori, emerging as the Divine image Obatala once wreaked in us. Animated by the breath of Olodumare, we are ignited in the glare of Iwori's challenge to transform, reborn in passion as a fully realized human being.

Odi

Cyclical time means that all is eventually reborn, in one way or another. In Ifá, the concept of reincarnation (Atunwa) is also present as a rebirth within a life cycle and into a new and separate life cycle with its own identity.

In Ifá, nothing is created or destroyed in the natural world. Rather, all that is has been transformed from something else and will be again, in a continuous cycle of rebirth. The perfect example is the one discussed earlier—the creation of humanity. Obatala made the forms of primordial human beings from clay. As in the Biblical Creation narrative, water was mixed with the earth's dirt and molded to create a kind of homunculus, a representation of what was to be transformed by the breath of Olodumare. In this instance, the transformation of the substance is accomplished by the Divine breath and the implantation of the Ori, the Divine kernel within humanity.

Yet, Odi also represents the physical act of birthing and female reproductive organs, referring to the animal reality of reproduction and the nurturing of new life within the human female's body. The womb is the place of transformation in which something that exists is changed to become something else entirely.

This womb is Odi, where all is reborn eternally and simultaneously, confounding the Western concept of time and a fixed moment of creative action on the part of the Divine. In the world of the Odi, creation is ongoing and uninterrupted, its primordial layer only the beginning of the Divine project of transforming matter into something new. The implication is progressive improvement and perfection. Matter that is not serving its purpose is transmuted. It becomes something new, improved, and closer to fulfilling its original purpose as laid out in the mind of Olodumare.

Iwori and Odi

While Iwori tends to a purely metaphysical characterization, Odi adds carnality in the presence of the womb. Representing both physical birth and continual cycles of rebirth, Odi connects reincarnation (re-fleshing) as linked to conventional physical birth and possibly even analogous to it.

Iwori transforms via the Ori, and Odi does the same but with a markedly different focus. While Iwori's gaze sparks transformation in the individual, Odi represents all birth and rebirth and the cyclical nature of time. As part of this schema, reincarnation is inevitable as only one consideration to consider while reflecting on the nature of rebirth as an eternal, unbroken series of cycles.

These circles of time revolve even in the world of linear time. Each minute contains 60 seconds; each hour 60 minutes. Each follows the next, with the week ending in Omega and beginning the next day in Alpha. While we may not acknowledge this reality, it is clear that time is cyclical. Even if we do not want that to be true, disguising time's circular, cyclical nature with all manner of fancy dress worthy of a naked Emperor, it's clear we know on some level that cyclical is what time has always been.

As Odi presides over our endless, eternal cycles, Iwori transforms the transformed, perfecting and refining human potential as it moves through time, ever-revolving and evolving, growing, and shrinking, being born and dying. Because no state of being is fixed in this model, all of life is a transformation process governed by Divine imperatives characterized as metaphysical concepts —and in Odi's case, a physical hybrid.

Both Iwori and Odi are concerned with transformation but in distinctly different ways. Iwori's penetrating gaze transforms by ignition of the Ori in its integrated state. Odi, on the other hand, recycles, recreating everything that exists anew in all the cycles of its life. This is as true of human beings as anything else in Creation.

Odi is "the seal," representing the female reproductive organs. However, those organs are only the "accident"—the mask that conceals the true face of the form in Aristotelian thinking—beneath which the truth rests, awaiting exposure. The accident reminds us of the function of the form. Because in the case of Odi, we are talking about cyclical rebirth or transformation, the seal of Odi provides a convenient symbol for the cycles of life and the earth. The process of rebirth is a transformation of another kind. While the transformation of Iwori is a fire, bending but not breaking the stuff of humanity, it eternally works the human soul through its destiny.

In the question of transformation, Odi's womb is life itself. But it is also the mind of Olodumare, in which Creation is conceived and then born, midwifed into being by co-creator, Obatala.

Rethink, Recycle, Rebirth

In Ifá cosmology, all is reborn. Starting at the moment of Creation, nothing is static. Nothing is complete. Nothing is perfected, and everything is subject to change. Unlike the Biblical Creation account, Ifá admits that Creation was formed from existing substance. The raw material was there. However, as with the forms of humans created by Obatala, the breath of the Divine was required to animate it.

Thus, Odi stands as the Divine imperative to rethink, recycle, and rebirth as an eternal renovation project, ever perfecting what is. Just as human followers of Ifá seek to perfect themselves by integrating their thoughts and emotions toward regulation and seeking the advice of the Orisha, all Creation is a work in progress. Eternity is long, so there is no excuse not to choose devotion to self-improvement. Because every transformation you make is a transformation that impacts the whole, when all Creation is engaged in the act of eternal transformation, there's no static field. Change is inevitable and mandated by the Creator as the whole truth about Creation—that the Creator's work is never done.

Iwori's gaze penetrates the cycles of this life. We continue to transform and become the people we seek to be in this life. In the lives to come, Odi is the womb from which we continually spring, ever perfecting and participating in perfection as subjects of an evolving Creation.

You will recall that we discussed the evolving nature of Odù Ifá in Chapter Six, with ese being added as the Orisha speak to the Babalawos/Iyalawos, revealing more about the relationship between Olodumare and the people of Ifá. Like the Ifá model of Creation, nothing is written in stone. Nothing is ever written down. It is memorized, added to, reinterpreted, and recast, ever-transforming as we transform.

The world of Ifá and its complex thought is governed by change, improvement, and transformation that move the material world closer to the intended model of Olodumare. In this process, humanity acts as co-creator, fitting the two halves of the great gourd back together. That wholeness is the intended relationship. It is the realization of Olodumare's dreams and eternal building project of humanity at the side of the Divine in common purpose.

Atunwa — The Recycled Soul

The concept of reincarnation in Ifá is very different from our conception in the West, which follows a loosely Eastern model. For us, reincarnation means returning to the earthly plane—whether consciously or unconsciously—as an ethereal soul inhabiting other people's bodies in other ages. This process is said to mitigate karmic obligations accumulated, leading us to Nirvana (the soul's perfection and release from "samsara"—the existential wheel).

In Ifá, the concept of reincarnation is rooted in individual choice. The Ori, the seat of the intellect and destiny, is the seat of this choice. This is the goal of divination—to illuminate the sacred Ori (the Orisha within) with the limitless wisdom of the spirit world. In pursuing the directives and guidance of divination, Ifá followers learn how to live in fidelity to their revealed destiny, fostering its direction and nurturing their understanding of it.

The ideal of Ifá, as in many other religions, is abundance, happiness, and a long life lived well. But that can only happen in Ifá when the practitioner is in tune with the Ori and the destiny it encapsulates. In this life, we choose our destinies by following the Sixteen Commandments. We heed the work of divination and the guidance of the Orisha through the Babalawo/Iyalawo. In following faithfully and practicing the orthopraxy prescribed by divination, the practitioner's soul is transformed, prepared for the reality of Atunwa and the destined evolution of the soul.

In the soul's future journey, the transformation of Odi, both physical and metaphysical, joins the work of Iwori, recycling and reusing the eternal soul. Duly formed in material life, the soul ventures forward into lives unknown, both in spirit and body. The mystery of a Creation that is ongoing, eternal, and cyclical is a journey of the human soul through the cycles of time, bound to sub-cycles that govern the conduct of that soul. Revolving and evolving, Atunwa is humanity's partnership with time, the soul submitting to the reality of Atunwa as the nature of the Created Order. Never completed, ever-evolving, all that is created is endlessly perfected and eternally ignited by the fire that changes but does not destroy.

Next, let us move into the second section of the Odù Ifá, reviewing the first two of the group in the next chapter.

Chapter 8: Odù Ifá II, Part One — Irosun and Oronwin

The framework of destiny is known in the Ori and revealed through the practice of divination. However, the realization of destiny is embodied by the practitioner. We choose to realize our potential or choose to reject it. That brings us to Irosun, the Odù of potential's fulfillment.

Irosun

Irosun concerns with the bold realization of potential, but it also means multiplication and increases. What is being increased is understanding, the qualities prescribed in the Sixteen Commandments, and the follower's adherence to the Ori's promptings. Once transformed by the fiery gaze of Iwori in submission to the cyclical leadings of Odi, Irosun goads the follower toward increase/multiplication.

Increase/multiplication can mean anything, and depending on the cycle of life we find ourselves in, different priorities at different times. We might find a cycle of increase applies to money, wisdom, knowledge, patience, compassion, or holiness. Ori's urgings may remind us of areas we need to increase toward realizing our destiny at any point in our lives. Potential has many faces in human life. We model it in many ways, from physical strength to intelligence. Moreover, in Irosun, we meet the archetype who reminds us that our potential is never entirely realized. Eternity, remember, is a long time; however, that does not imply there is any sitting on our Irosun laurels!

Ori will make sure of that, and to keep pace with Ori, in fidelity to the destiny it is the guardian of, followers of Ifá are ever urged to "check themselves." Irosun implies that seeking potential in ourselves is how we push ourselves toward destiny and our work with the Divine. It's easy to become spiritually stagnant in many religious systems. But in Ifá, the driving force of divination and its connection to Ori creates a purpose-built vehicle that prevents such stagnation. The believer is part of a system that seeks communal orthopraxy within a religious framework. It's about what you think and what you do due to what you think. It's very much a works-based religion, demanding something from followers toward enhancing the whole, including the other half of the gourd, the spirit world.

The Blood

What Irosun also means in Yoruba is "menstrual blood." In that blood, present in its monthly cycles, is an elaboration on Atunwa because Atunwa means a specific type of reincarnation in Ifá, linked to the ancestors through the bonds of flesh (and blood).

While reincarnation is not strictly linked to family ties, Ifá says this is usually the case, with Atunwa primarily limited to family. The blood that once flowed through the ancestors' veins, in this way, is perpetuated. And the bonds of family are, as well. Blood is potential, and that is especially true of menstrual blood.

Menstrual blood is the cyclical shedding of the womb's lining, occurring on twenty-one to twenty-eight-day cycles throughout a woman's life from adolescence to menopause. Descending from Odi (the womb), this blood enters the material world as potential. When the blood does not come as it usually does, another kind of potential is being realized—that of birth.

Family blood and menstrual blood coalesce in Irosun as the ink creating the soul's road map to and through eternity. In blood is the stuff of life. In blood is the DNA of family lineage. And in the blood is the material maternal home of the soul in transit, ready to be born.

As we are talking about menstrual blood, we must also talk about women and their role in the life of Ifá. There is a remarkable contrast between the metaphor of menstrual blood as a symbol of potential in Ifá and the horror with which it is greeted in the Monotheistic Faiths. Without much detail, the Hebrew women of the Bronze Age were relegated to tents when they menstruated. And the Christian Church persisted in rites to "re-church" women after birth, as though birth had somehow sullied their bodies, well into the 1980s and later (see resources). While routinely framed as a "blessing," the churching of women was concerned primarily with ritual purity after its predecessor: Faith.

The positioning of women as metaphors for potential and the cyclical nature of life is a primordial response to women's reproductive functions, one of which is menstruation. While viewed as contaminating in some religious traditions, in Ifá, menstruation is viewed as a partner in the progress of time itself. A metaphor for time's cyclical nature, the potential of the blood is human—spiritually, intellectually, and materially. This conforms to a much older tradition of framing the female sex. Mysteriously bringing forth life in humanity's earliest days, women were viewed with reverence and fear. Whatever made the sunrise and set, it seemed too early for humans that women probably had something to do with it. The goddesses of the world's ancient cultures and the female Orisha speak to the power once held in menstrual blood and women as bearers of life. This ancient value in Ifá frames "woman" as the human embodiment of potential, stewards of both the womb and the blood that issues from it, representing potential and renewal.

Irosun has a negative side and, as usual, has to do with resisting one's destiny. When the practitioner works against the destiny outlined in the Ori and discovers in divination, the potential is choked off. Potential is refused. Even the blood of one's family and the ancestors' guidance is refused. However, who could refuse the riches of the past, present, and future in the potential the Ori holds as Divine legacy? It seems foolhardy, and perhaps that answers any questions about how it is that Ifá has survived eight millennia as a system of Faith. What works for people is usually continued, creating and recreating, birthing potential, and reincarnating it in Atunwa.

Potential in Flesh and Blood

Ifá's dedication to the community and the families that constitute it is clear in the conception of reincarnation in Atunwa. Blood is the potential of the flesh. The incarnation of potential relies on blood that springs from a font of relatedness. In this, the ancestors are serviced.

But all blood is potential in Irosun. The menstrual blood being the potential for life shed each month, is tied to the cycles of Creation, making Irosun that living womb of all lives that are, have been, and will be.

Inseparable from the living being, except in the monthly shedding of the womb's lining, the blood is the potential for graduation from the earthly to the spiritual. In the incarnate human is the potential for an eternity of spiritual evolution. This evolution is served both in the living human's development and the development of the soul liberated to its destiny in Atunwa.

Oronwin

Because the Odù Ifá's role is to define existence and the energies impacting it, members of the Faith are prepared for all contingencies, including the unexpected. This is the archetype of life represented by Orunwin—sudden, unexpected change.

This is where the Odù Ifá veers into the realm of Physics, specifically, the chaos that is matter's underlying nature. While we all like to believe that the universe, the world, and our lives are well ordered, Physics teaches that the truth is very different. The closer we examine the surface of things, the more chaos is seen beneath its flimsy veneer. Yet the more distance we place between ourselves and apparently unrelated, random events, the more orderly they appear. This is the effect described by Orunwin, which teaches perspective and the laudable trait of equanimity. Orunwin also instructs that all is not what it seems, demanding that the observer consider what is being experienced from the standpoint of impassive observation.

Our overthinking makes us see the chaos beneath the surface when we obsess about unexpected events—life's curveballs. In our zeal to make a difficult or unpleasant situation "go away," we major in the minors, picking problems apart until there is nothing left to pick, yet being no closer to any solution.

Alternatively, putting some distance between ourselves and what's happening allows us to see things as they are. What might appear chaotic up close will seem less so when viewed with detachment and realism.

Chaos Theory according to the Ifá

Chaos Theory (a branch of mathematics) proposes that combined chaos and order are the whole truth about reality. As stated above, what looks chaotic in proximity looks orderly from a distance. However, when chaos is considered from a mathematical perspective, the universe unfolds as it should, following a determined pathway that we perceive as chaos. But that is because we do not understand what we are looking at without doing the math.

The systems of the natural world are deeply deterministic. Yet, small changes to those systems can produce adverse effects over time. The Butterfly Effect, first described by meteorologist Edward Lorenz in 1961, analogizes this effect. Lorenz found that even minute errors in calculations when forecasting the weather threw the entire system out of whack. Just as a butterfly flapping its wings halfway around the world might be responsible for a hurricane, deviations in orderly systems can create ever-accumulating anomalies that result in similar disruptions.

Similarly, small disruptions of the destiny contained in the Ori of the individual threaten the integrity of the destiny's trajectory. The butterfly wings that buffet the world's stability are also capable of causing chaos in our lives—at least it looks like chaos, close up. The chaos just beneath the surface of life, the little bumps and grinds that distress and confuse us, is order asserting itself in ways we cannot predict. The death of a loved one, a sudden layoff from work, illness, and betrayal are part of life but appear to us as chaotic interruptions in our personal, calmly flowing rivers.

According to the Ifá, Chaos Theory is the peaceful meeting of life where it stands, understanding that everything happens as part of our destiny. Observed for what they are, the shocks of life are absorbed. When we look at what has happened in our lives as part of a greater story, not a personal insult or a life-destroying catastrophe, we're better able to see the order in chaos and, conversely, the chaos that serves order.

Returning to the Sixteen Commandments of Ifá, it is clear that their object is not orthopraxy for its own sake or for that of some arcane ideology—which is of little interest to the practice of Ifá. Instead, the Sixteen Commandments serve order by urging the faithful to act toward the smooth functioning of the communal system by avoiding disruptive behaviors because, in the model of the commandments, chaos is provoked by deviations in the conduct of life that creates hurt, misunderstanding, and even violence.

While under the calm surface of an orderly society, chaos teems as it serves that order, ever moving toward the solutions it was intended to create, its perceived presence in our lives is still serving that same order—in death, misfortune, illness, job loss, and disappointment. These contingencies are not essentially chaotic; they are simply part of an orderly reality in which chaos is part of a whole, reproducing reality as we know it.

Change and Equanimity

Oronwin provides perspective to supplicants who come to divination in times of flux and upheaval. Change means different things to different people. Some people provoke change voluntarily, knowing that change is needed. However, most of us find change threatening. We are creatures who like the familiar. A two-week vacation is just about right for most of us. Most of us want to return to our own beds after a vacation—too much change.

Change demands adaptation. When it is an unforeseen change of whatever kind, the ability to confront it makes us resilient. We learn from surviving, not from contentment. Contentment is the reward you receive for surviving.

Increasingly, societies everywhere have become less resilient due to an unwillingness to absorb change by adapting to it. Change and adaptation can take numerous forms, from personal tragedy to natural disasters. But to survive, we must be prepared to accept change as a challenge.

We adapt to changing from the comfort and dependence of childhood to transition into the adult world. This transition is common to all of us, with exceptions to the rule that only serve to prove it. Yet, when a change arises like a pandemic, do we accept the temporary inconvenience represented by mandates to mask or distance socially, or do we rebel against them? Which is the more common response?

Fortunately, most choose acceptance in the face of change, which comes with the inconvenience. That is how we survive. Even if we find the change abhorrent (occupation, war), we must learn to be in the experience as ourselves, fully engaged with the moment and not attempting to disrupt it with personal interest. In moments of great change, there is no personal interest. There's communal integrity that serves the desired outcome: Survival.

The perspective offered by Orunwin concerning change is that of equanimity. Change will happen. It is inevitable—and the choices you make when determining fidelity to the destiny held within the Ori. Thus, Orunwin counsels the type of acceptance that invests the mind in its own happiness. This is equanimity.

Equanimity places the person's response above the disruption encountered in the magnitude of importance. It is not the condition that matters where equanimity is concerned; it's the individual's response to that condition. All things have equal value in life and must be seen as parts of a whole which is the big picture.

The ancient Stoics believed that equanimity brought happiness, placing its practice high on its list of personal virtues, and virtue, they believed, was enough to keep you happy. This is similar to the idea of Oronwin in the Odù Ifá. Oronwin is the energy of change, and the change in Ifá is a challenge—a rite of passage that demands a response indicating your maturity as a human being. That maturity, in Orunwin, is seen in the ability to step back and consider the place of each change in life, whether cyclical (adulthood, birth, death, marriage) or unique incidents (sudden economic or social loss, accidents, ill-health). This is summed up in the character trait of equanimity.

Ifá's teachings in the archetypes expressed in the Odù Ifá are oriented toward self-command and exemplary action. Orthopraxy being central to the practice of the religion is only possible in a person who has learned what it is to be genuinely and deeply human. In Ifá, that deep humanity is the centrality of the spirit in incarnated life. The Ori must be followed, the intellect developed, and the spirit attuned to its destiny to serve that spirit. That destiny is to serve the whole great gourd.

Imagine the Ifá concept of Atunwa for a moment. Imagine the cycles of life being eternal with the souls of the Faithful learning through eternity, acting justly through eternity, and adding ese to the Odù Ifá through eternity. Change is part of these life cycles after life, simultaneous and yet, removed. Change is the nature of life, with the death of the physical body being the greatest change we will ever experience after that first moment outside the birth canal, dripping with Irosun's potential.

A Big Change

Death is feared by most of us. It is the unknown, and, like change, humans are not crazy about what they do not know or understand. However, like all the other life changes, death must be accepted. One has no alternative. Death is the end.

Thus, equanimity becomes Ifá's means of teaching the Faithful about the biggest change of all, the death of the material body. In Ifá, there's no dichotomy between the body and spirit. The spirit of humanity is divinely implanted as a part of the body. It is unique to the individual and not fixed. On the contrary, an individual's destiny may be changed due to their actions. The Ori of an individual may be improved or degraded. It is entirely the individual's decision what to do about themselves. But the best choice is made abundantly clear to the practitioner by the community around them and the people in it.

In the metaphors and ideas explored in this chapter, you have discovered a practical and constructive heart to the Ifá faith and the ultimate gift of divination. The Odù Ifá's lessons in Irosun and Oronwin are about the cycle of life itself, reaching out to the individual member to prepare them in this life for all that will come. In all our cycles, we honor and increase our potential. And in all our eternities, we change and transform profoundly.

Chapter 9: Odù Ifá II, Part Two — Obara and Okanran

In this, we come to the concept of inner character. Starting with Obara (strength) and concluding with Okanran (humility), there is an interplay between the two qualities we can all learn something powerful from.

Obara

Strength can be a confusing term, muddled with culture. For some, it means winning at all costs and coming out on top; collateral damage damned. However, that is the negative face of Obara, the Odù/archetype of strength. In Ifá, the ego is born in the will to personal power, which precludes humility.

The imposition of one's will to prevail is the opposite of humility, which seeks its place among many. Ego demands its place above all. It is easy to see this in community elevation in the Ifá Faith, but in Ifá, Obara is also the birthplace of humility.

Having already irritated Olodumare with their rude, dismissive habits, human beings would be best served by not mistaking strength for self-interest. For nothing in Ifá may be had at the expense of others when the religion's Commandments are followed. And no living human being can ever match the strength of the Creator.

Yet, humanity can be a bit pigheaded, so the idea that we are "bigger than God" pervades at certain moments, leading us to behave irrationally and counter to reality. It's difficult for us to concede that the heavens are not solely concerned with us, personally. We cannot help believing, it seems, that nature was created solely for our cavalier use.

Egotism is anathema to the practice of Ifá for all the reasons you have been reading about. Odù Ifá, working in tandem with Ifá divination practices, is intended to divest followers of this all-too-human tendency, replacing it with the true strength of which Obara is the universal archetype. When the elevation of the self is reformed, humility has space to develop. But only when this transformation takes place can that true strength take root.

The Strength to Confront Reality

Lately, the reality is something else we humans do not seem to much care for. And yet, there it is: The elephant in the room, relieving itself of all our confabulating fun. However, the reality is the truth, and we may only be transformed by that truth by confronting it.

Confronting reality is perhaps the birthplace of the equanimity we read of in the last chapter, where the rubber meets the road, and we accept change by keeping calm and carrying on. It is a scary thing to do, but we all must confront reality. We need to admit that life does not always run as though on a conveyor belt, conveniently sending us off on our way in only one predictable direction. We need to make peace with the fact that we will die, we are finite, and our fleshly existence is not the nexus of reality.

We must confront and discern reality for the demands of a future of well-developed equanimity. Learning that you cannot always get what you want takes longer for some than others. But learn you must to survive and thrive and graduate through the cycles of your eternal life to spiritual maturity. And within Obara is the answer, which is the transformation of the ego, making space for humility to arise and overwhelm it. This is one of the principal lessons of life for the Ifá. Humility is at the center of their practice as the connective tissue of a communally ordered society.

Character Is Humility

Only when the ego is tamed can space for humility be made. The ego has sharp elbows, demanding as much space as possible. Ego spreads, making a two-seater on the bus a one-seater.

When the ego is duly tamed, it is contained to its rightful place, not spreading out to command more space than it's due but ordered and managed to make space for humility. As you read earlier, humility is a key human characteristic prized in Ifá. Humility causes us to consider the other side of arguments, take other people's concerns seriously, and factor their right to peace and well-being into our words and actions.

Humility is the core of a good character, engaged with the project of being decent, respectful, and considerate of the needs of others. When ego spreads itself out, taking up more space than a single person has any right to, there is no space for humility, self-reflection, or self-correction. Humility is elbowed out.

In Okanran, we explore the universal energy of humility and how its formation depends on knowing Obara well and realistically.

Okanran

In Ifá, tutu represents the balancing of emotion and thought. This is required to free human beings from the mindlessness of the lizard brain (the amygdala), which is the reactive, primitive part of the brain. When tutu is achieved, thoughts and emotions inform one another, with thought tempering emotion and vice versa.

The perfect illustration of what happens when thought and emotion are disconnected is found in the Third Reich. As the extermination of those deemed "the enemy" was the goal, the enemy's dehumanization was required to meet that goal. To do this, the Nazis engaged in the intellectualization of genocide, rejecting any emotional input as to the humanity of the people they were torturing and killing.

When the intellect is unmoored from emotion, robotic evil is set loose. Similarly, reactive outbursts, arguments, physical violence, and other social evils result when emotion is unmoored from the intellect. Thus, the two must be integrated for the human organism to be balanced and actively human. Imbalance is yet another deviation from the original plan set forth by Olodumare.

Okanran's metaphor is of one who humbly beats floormats, cleaning them of dirt. This precision in describing the trait of humility is breathtaking. When we think of the one who beats the mat to loosen embedded dirt, we think of humility—the performance of unseen and undervalued actions toward the well-being of the mat-beater and others.

The mat-beater benefits as richly as those who use the mat. And so, at the base of humility is a constructive self-interest. Life is just happier sitting on a well-beaten mat. The mat-beater is as comfortable as the others sitting on the mat. In truth, what is being beaten is the ego, as constructive self-interest includes others in the beneficial outfall.

Okanran stands as the solution to the out-of-proportion ego drive. While the ego looks out at the world and sees it as its oyster, humility does the same and realizes it's part of a greater whole. Humility does not presume primacy, whereas ego demands it at the expense of others.

When the follower of Ifá is led to the realization that the ego is standing in the way of spiritual development, Okanran instigates the cycle that provokes it. The ego must be contained for humility to rush into the space the ego formerly had "hogged."

The negative aspect of Okanran results from failing to balance emotions with thoughts. The first line of attack is balancing thoughts and emotions, strengthening the Ori, and growing humility to its rightful stature.

When humility is grown, life is renewed. We arrive at the understanding that our subjective reading of the world around us, placing ourselves at its center, is delusional. Here, we truly confront reality, looking into its depths to discover the truth: That we are part of something much larger than us or our restless egos. The next cycle of life is freshly realized as humility slides into its seat and begins to grow its influence.

Iwa Pele

Good character is rooted in humility, and in Ifá, a good (or gentle) character is called "Iwa Pele." Throughout the Odù, Ifá is referenced, guiding to achieving Iwa Pele. As you have seen, this guidance is summarized in the Sixteen Commandments, making clear what one of good character does and does not do.

Iwa Pele seeks humility but also generosity, wisdom, truth, and patience. Good character is rooted in humility because humility understands that it needs to grow to fill the character of the human it is seeded in. That growth feeds the quest for the other virtues Iwa Pele thirsts after to nourish itself as a spirit prepared for life.

However, the cultivation of Iwa Pele is also for the sake of the community central to the practice of Ifá. A community characterized by all these virtues is happy and mindful of others and spirit. Such a community attracts the favor of the ancestors, Orisha and Olodumare.

When these gentle virtues are practiced, the community learns the meaning of peace, preparing the way of the Iwa Pele to the life of the spirit, informed, and sanctified by Odù Ifá. And community is the model of Faith. Creating human communities of Iwa Pele and restoring community between both halves of the cosmic gourd paves the way for eternally revolving cycles of transformative change.

Humility in Ifá means something more than it means to most of us. Ifá's vision of humility encompasses the understanding that we are not islands and do not succeed because of our inimitable personal virtue. We succeed as part of a community of actors participating as one to create that success.

Yet, something the West will not understand is that Ifá does not strictly adhere to the concept of an individualized soul. In Ifá, while Ori is assigned to the individual, it is but an emanation of Olodumare, the essence of the Divine in our mortal bodies and Ori. Humility, in Ifá, is the setting of the human ego within a great whole of which she is neither better nor worse, lesser, or greater. Ifá teaches that all is one thing, emanating from the same Divine source. In that model, humility is the conduit by which humanity might again reflect the Divine intention for it.

Okanran is about knowing our place in the grand cosmology of things, not pretending we have any special rights exceeding or challenging those of others. The mat-beater's humility is toward the benefit of the whole, ensuring it does its part for the integrity of all in Olodumare.

Ifá Will Mend It

"It will not be spoiled in our own time.
It will not be spoiled in our own time.
The world will not be spoiled in our own time.
Ifá will mend it."

Wande Abimbola

Ògúnwáńdé "Wande" Abímbọ́lá is a Nigerian academician and professor of Yoruba language and literature. He is also a Chief, installed by the Babalawos of Yorubaland, and his definition of Ifá is that of a salvific philosophy of living that is Divinely mandated.

Wande Abimbola teaches language and literature in Nigeria.
https://unsplash.com/photos/wiUl_NyafcY

"Ifá will mend it" is a strong and unequivocal statement, and again, the daily righteousness of Haredi Jews comes to mind, with their assertion that the practice of the 613 mitzvot will restore Creation. The implication in Ifá is the same, stating that by practicing the Sixteen Commandments and following the teachings offered in divination, the grand project of restoring the integrity of the cosmos will be achieved.

While many religions feature cleansing destruction, positing that Creation will rise from its ashes, Ifá chooses the "home improvements" method. Instead of tearing the whole thing down, it seeks to mend the structure, restoring it to its original condition.

In Judaism, this means the practice of ethically driven, humble living, unmoved by the promptings of the restless human ego. However, this humble living is not intended as a sacrifice or cage in Ifá. Living in a community and in mindfulness of that community's well-being is a template for a satisfying life on earth. The practice of Ifá benefits every living human and all Creation. It is the practice of living in the moment for the future and the past because past, present, and future are all one thing held within a now that determines the health of the integrated whole. In this model, the now is the pivot point.

That pivot point is most dynamic in the practice of divination. As discussed, divination is a guide, allowing supplicants seeking the support of the Babalawo/Iyalawo to impact the progress of their destinies by following the advice of the Odù indicated and the priest's interpretations of it. This agency on the part of the followers of Ifá is the exercise of free will within a communal framework. Within that framework, the individual seeks the most beneficial action for their and the community's well-being.

The now, in Ifá, is part of the eternal revolution of time, with past, present, and future interacting in mysterious ways that result in destinies realized. "Ifá will mend it," as Chief Wande wrote, is a statement set in the future. Like an affirmation, it's a confident statement of a future reality. Ifá has been mending the world for 8,000 years. It's mending the world now. It will mend the world tomorrow. Chief Wande's statement rejects the eschatology of other religions, placing the world's fate firmly in the hands of the living and the religion they follow.

The archetype of humility, Okanran, is a thematic pillar of Ifá, linking all its complex themes back to a single quality. The mending of the world depends on humility, and Ifá acts not as a private club for those who practice a religion to soothe their souls. Ifá acts as a gift to the world, the actions of the faithful mending what has become obsolete or damaged. Nothing in Creation is beyond repair. It's only in need of the love of communal action, directed to the healing of Creation.

The negative manifestation of Obara (strength/ego) is conquered by the ascension of the mat-beating Okanran, as dust is removed so that all might again enjoy the mat in humility. As Chief Wande has written, Ifá will mend it.

In the next chapter, we move on to the Odù Ifá III.

Chapter 10: Odù Ifá III, Part One — Ogunda and Osa

In this chapter, we will examine Ogunda and Osa, the first two Odù s of Odù Ifá III. The theme of transformative change is central to this chapter, with Ogunda and Osa serving that project in their respective and complementary functions. (NB: The themes are the same as those found in Chapter Six, with Ogbe and Oyeku, with the energies expressed in the respective Odu personified somewhat differently. It is interesting to note that distinctions like these are part of the didactic process of Ifá divination.)

Ogunda

Ogunda is an archetype of transformation, but in that archetype is the ability to remove obstacles. What is created by this natural energy is the creation of opportunity and the enabling of new cycles of growth and personal development.

Many of the obstacles Ogunda removes are self-imposed. Human beings and the egos we struggle with can lead us into all kinds of behaviors damaging to ourselves, our communities, and our destinies.

Most religions speak of intemperate behavior as detrimental to the human soul. Ifá discusses this behavior as preventing the Ori from operating as intended to and interfering with and corroding the community's well-being. Overindulgence in alcohol, drug use, fighting, and other bad human habits has a distinct ripple effect recognized in this communally focused Faith.

Ogunda speaks directly to the practitioner's connection to the Ori and all the things that stand in the way of that crucial connection. Ego is one of the great obstacles—especially to the growth of humility (as discussed in the last chapter). When permitted to explode to the degree at which the self is the pre-eminent, ego leads to aberrant behaviors that are disruptive and damaging to the self and others.

Ogunda's role in transformation is to clear away the obstacles that prevent us from moving through eternity unimpeded by negative habits of thought and emotion. In the integrated Ori, the seat of destiny is cleansed of roadblocks and debris, allowing the free movement of the intellect, emotions, and spirit toward destiny.

Patience and Self-Control

Chief among the attributes taught by Odù Ogunda are patience and self-control. Patience is a function of the balanced individual. Emotion is tempered by thought, and thought is filtered through emotion. Considered are not only the emotions of the person seeking out Ogunda but also those of others, in the family and community. When patience is fostered in the self, perspective is reached, and the ability to see clearly without bias or self-deception is achieved.

Self-control is a tremendous problem for many people. We do not think before we act, and we don't question the validity of our thoughts. In the heat of the moment, we rarely take a moment to interrogate where our thoughts are leading us. However, to be humble, we must. Humility is the breath we take before white-hot rage spills out from the mouth, burning all it touches.

Ogunda is a proving ground for the human's command of Ori. To honor and live in the trajectory of our true destiny, our egotistical self-indulgence and self-obsession must be subjected to the backhoe of Ogunda. If it is not serving your destiny, it's getting leveled.

Self-control is not biting the tongue; self-control is a level-headed self-examination that does not start seconds before a potential interpersonal conflict. The ability to control emotions and meet discord with equanimity and placid confidence is an everyday discipline practiced for a lifetime. It gets easier, but because we are human, the work is never done.

Back to Iwa Pele

As you learned in the last chapter, Iwa Pele is a good or gentle character. This is another pillar of Ifá. A person of good character is alive to the Ori, and their destiny is born within her.

A person of gentle character can also better control their emotions and is endlessly patient with the curveballs of life and the people who throw them. This person understands that everything changes and evolves and that the fewer roadblocks there are to impede evolutionary change, the better off Creation will eventually be. Ifá will mend it.

In Ogunda is the training of the character. Turning the human tendency to overindulge in bad habits toward the nobler pursuit of following and realizing Ori is the fruit of Ogunda, the remover of obstacles and the creator of opportunities and new horizons.

Fundamental to Iwa Pele is the temperament because it is in the temperament that we see the truth about people. We see their maturity or lack thereof in their ability to control emotional reactions. In the human temperament are the makings of leadership.

As you are reading, hopefully, you're connecting with the interplay of the energies represented by the Odùs that we are discussing. As you can see, what is emerging is a snapshot of the Odù Ifá's mission: To teach followers the lessons learned by the ancestors and collected by the Babalawo/Iyalawo as templates for living. Every Odù has a specific energy, discussing similar and overlapping themes. Within each energy is the vibration of every variation and what it means in terms of living with integrity in the Ifá model. And all this is to transform the follower's life to be in line with the purpose of destiny, both collective and individual. In each Odùs is a world of self-development and information about how we might better ourselves for the good of all.

Iwa Pele is the goal of all Ifá followers. In Ogunda, the patience and self-control needed to achieve the status of Iwa Pele are nurtured by clearing away what's impeding progress. That brings us to Osa, which is another clearing away with explosive implications.

Osa

All that occurs in life cannot be traced to our own actions. Saying that is true is repeating fiction. Reality precludes the fantastical belief that we control it. We control our reactions to what happens but do not control reality. We are the subjects of reality, and we choose how we respond to that subject status. That is our locus of control—our response.

Osa is the stuff we have no control over. It is a riverbank breaking, forcing water into the street, pushing vehicles with its fearsome strength. Osa is the thunderstorm, the chunks of hail that dent the roofs of cars. Osa is an earthquake that levels a town. Osa is the unexpected, the catastrophic.

However, in cataclysm, there is the shock of rebirth. When all has been suddenly torn down, there is no choice but to build back up, which is one of the tenets of Ifá. All that has been made is subject to change. Nothing is complete. Nothing is perfect. Change does not stop. In the ever-evolving cosmos of Ifá, what is no longer serving its purpose is transformed, recycled, and reused. It's restored to more closely reflect the Divine Will's original intention.

Cataclysm as Revolution

Osa, as mentioned above, is the unexpected cataclysm. Just when you think all your ducks are in a tidy row, along comes Osa to disavow your silly assumptions. In our comfort and self-congratulation for how great our lives our, we forget that anything can happen. We forget that our presumed virtue is not a bulwark against the unpredictable.

Major illness may be more in the realm of Oronwin, who is the chaos serving order. While unexpected, it comes from within. It comes from our destiny, and how we choose to confront a major illness is where the learning takes place. On the other hand, Osa is entirely external to us, crashing into our well-ordered lives like a rampaging bull.

Anything can happen in a natural world increasingly being challenged by human activity, giving rise to extreme weather of all kinds. The natural world is rebelling, dealing out punishing hurricanes to destructive tsunamis, and we are part of that world. Intrinsic to, yet in awe of it, we find ourselves in the path of the natural world's rebellion against us.

And when it hits us, the world we know that feeds us, waters us, and is our home is suddenly an enemy, threatening to remove us from its surface. The standard response is "Why?" "Why me?" "Why here?" There is nothing we can do. We either pack up and get out of the path of whatever natural disaster is bearing down on us, or we stay, taking our chances. The latter option was taken by many in New Orleans, Los Angeles, as Hurricane Katrina bore down on Crescent City on August 29,

2005. New Orleans residents had been through it all before. Many hurricanes had buffeted the city over its long life and reside in the recent memory of residents. Some New Orleanians felt that they knew the drill and had the lay of the land. They had their ducks in a row, and so, they stayed.

Many died. Many lost homes that had been in their families for generations. But almost two decades after the Federal Levee Disaster of New Orleans—a clue as to how chaos only serves order it recognizes as order—New Orleanians continue to sing:

"Meanwhile, you might as well have a good time.

Meanwhile, there may not be the next time.

Meanwhile, you better shake that pretty booty, baby."

- Ivan Neville, Dumphstahfunk

They continued to live, work and love in New Orleans, knowing that nature could have another go at them. And yet, there they are.

On the Worst Day of Your Life

Everyone holds a narrative about the worst day of their life in their mind. For most New Orleans residents, that was the day the levees broke. It was not enough that a Category 5 hurricane had descended on New Orleans. The levees, constructed by the supposedly competent Army Corps of Engineers, gave way under the onslaught of a powerful hurricane.

Thus, humanity failed to collaborate with nature by limiting its potential for destruction. Nature and its behaviors have no ethics, no morals, no thought. Nature is like the Divine in that respect. Its ways are not our ways. Yet, our ways did not serve the whole of nature on that fateful day by neglecting the human element—the residents of New Orleans.

No one can imagine living such a horrifying day as that day in New Orleans unless they were there. However, one can imagine the terror of all that water coming at them. We have seen the destruction water is capable of, especially when humans neglect to protect those most vulnerable.

Added to the terror of Katrina is the betrayal of other humans of a collective it deemed unworthy of government-funded protection in a hurricane-prone city. How could that day not have been the worst of your life? But Katrina's destruction lasted eight long days, causing almost 2,000 deaths and billions of dollars in damage.

Osa is the cataclysm, while Ogunda holds the key to survival. In the instance of Katrina, the equanimity brings those who survived the courage to go on. After seeing your city swamped, largely abandoned by the federal government, as human bodies floated in the engulfed streets, how do you go on? You just do it because the community is there, and it always will be as long as the land is above water.

As you can see, the energies described in this chapter are synchronous with those discussed in Ogbe and Oyeku in Chapter Six but with divergent energetic agendas. Unexpected change in Oyeku comes from within. In Osa, it is external. Similarly, Ogbe removes obstacles but trusts in service of following the promptings of destiny in the Ori. Ogunda removes obstacles expressed physically in corrosive habits that lead to disunity and dysfunction. The symbols are the same, but the agendas are different in energetic quality.

Meanwhile, back in New Orleans, the city may not have been renewed as hoped, but the culture of the community continues to thrive and grow, springing up from the cataclysm in triumphant joy. Survival is the necessity we must serve in confronting reality, and this is evident in the cultural and communal recovery from Katrina. None of this is attributable to anyone outside that community. All this was and has always been achieved by people who model equanimity as a way of life.

In the lyrics of the song "Meanwhile," shown at the beginning of this chapter, it's not difficult to sense the equanimity of a population accustomed to cataclysm. From Yellow Fever to Katrina, New Orleans has suffered numerous roundhouse kicks. However, through it all, the community has repeatedly risen up in music and culture, ever singing the song of destiny stuck in its throat.

Cyclical Cataclysm and Rebirth

New Orleans is easily identifiable as an icon of Black American culture. With its extraordinary legacy of Second Lines, Mardi Gras Indians, Louis Armstrong, and Little Wayne, the city is a cauldron of Black America's most vibrant links to Africa. Those links are apparent in Voudon, both practiced and celebrated in this majority Roman Catholic city. Hoodoo is also practiced as a living legacy rooted in the abuses of the plantation, some of which still stand in stately splendor to satisfy visitors' curiosity.

Within the cyclical cataclysms that mark New Orleans's long and checkered history are multiple rebirths that speak of an unbreakable spirit.

In that spirit are echoes of Ifá. Those echoes are in the patience, fortitude, and equanimity of a people apart, riding the chaos hiding beneath order like a streetcar. They get off at the next stop and join the Second Line parade, picking up the nearest tambourine.

And that is the combined lesson of Ogunda and Osa. With patience and self-control, we get off at the next stop and keep going in full command of our emotions. The past is over. There may not be a next time, but go on and shake that pretty booty because cycles come and go. Life cycles, falling and rising in cataclysmic succession as life leaps riotously from the rubble, which will soon be recycled. Trumpets blow— Tubas throb. The asphalt sings with dancing feet.

This is not to suggest that New Orleans is a microcosm of Ifá practice, but what is clear is that the spirit is there, in the people. No religion can live for 8,000 years and not become part of a people's DNA, both culturally and physically. Visit the Voodoo Temple on Rampart Street and see how true this is. Witness the survival of traditions originating in Haiti (the Second Line and shotgun houses, for starters). Experience people that will not stop dancing, singing, playing, creating, building up, and tearing down as the streets are full to the brim.

Cataclysm and rebirth are the nature of New Orleans, just as they are the nature of Ifá's cosmic gourd. Every catastrophic impact of nature results in its new growth, just as the people know in their souls.

Chapter 11: Odù Ifá III, Part Two — Ika and Oturupon

In the second part of our exploration Part III, we explore two Odu/archetypes, which speak to two opposed aspects of the human personality: Power and weakness. We will examine their energetic missions and the interplay between Ika and Oturopon.

Ika

In Ika, the Iwa Pele (good/gentle character) is transformed to become personal power. We all manifest personal power in different ways. In Ika, power is externalized in the invocation of wisdom in the spoken word. Personal power is still the act of affirming the self and its truths, but it is also speaking those truths as a public reflection of the self.

The self cannot be affirmed (entirely) from within. To achieve self-affirmation, a strong sense of self and one's relationship to the world is needed. Most of us, though, will not have such a sense of self until some point in our second decade. Others will not have this sense of self until much later. However, for the most part, we understand ourselves and where we stand in relation to the world and other people by looking at what is reflected by them. From the impressions of others and our interactions with them, we come to learn about ourselves and who we are. We find, as we grow, our power.

But Ika proposes that the person's truth is in the word and the wisdom that drives it. Arising from the Ashé, personal power is the ability to create and participate in change and to make things happen in the world around you.

We have yet to speak of Ashé in this book, but Ika is where Ashé is at its most powerful energetically, leading the believer toward the power within them. In the wisdom-informed word, Ashé is realized, and Ika is where that happens.

Personal power is what holds us all up, giving us the ability to walk down the street, interact with other people, and live our lives. However, personal power is so much more than being able to function in the world. In Ashé, personal power becomes almost material, manifesting as the development of wisdom made whole in the spoken word.

As a sign of power, the spoken word is not surprising from Ifá, a religion that relies on oral tradition to pass down its ancestral wisdom. Wisdom is collected to be shared, and when a written account may not be made, that wisdom must be spoken. In the Babalawo/Iyalawo, the collected wisdom of the ancestors is incarnated as a repository of the sum of Ifá's many gifts. That spoken word is the living voice of the ancestors and the Orisha, speaking as the attributes of a distant God.

Olodumare's Gift

Ashé is the same power that created everything in the universe. It is a direct infusion of the Divine Power into all humans, plants, rocks, water, and everything else. Ashé is the life force that animates and sustains us as creaturely beings. Without Ashé, nothing can exist. It is a Divine gift that lives in all and makes all live.

And Ashé is most powerfully manifested in the spoken word when it speaks in the ancestors' wisdom and acts in that same wisdom. Like the Ori, Ashé is specific to the person, organism, or object it animates. While part of something larger, like Ori, it is contained in its individuality (personal unit of consciousness).

With the gift of divination, Ashé is honored with wisdom, again emphasizing the importance of the practice. As Divine power (potential in the human), Ashé must be fed to become the authoritative voice it is intended to be. With the infusion of wisdom provided by divination, the believer grows in Ashé, reaching its full manifestation in the Ori's destiny.

Ika is where Ashé is grown in the power of the word. As the power of the word is the highest manifestation of Ashé, forming and realizing it is the source of healing and transformation. Ika's negative aspect is the tendency to abuse personal power to indulge in idle gossip at the expense of other people. However, the Ashé, which is well-formed in the wisdom and power of the word, is the true, positive Ashé allowing humanity the luxury of Divine power within a circumscribed theater—the word. From this theater proceeds power infused with wisdom, which brings forward the intentions of Olodumare for Creation's continuing and eternal evolution.

Oturopon

Oturopon is the energy of disease, especially infectious disease. However, it is also the energy of protection against disease. Ika's power is juxtaposed to the weakness inflicted by illness, striking us and laying us low. But the disease is a double-edged sword in the human organism. As we have seen with the pandemic, the immune system can become stronger when exposed to an infectious disease, preventing death and serious, long-term illness.

When COVID arrived, there was no vaccine for it—although science had been attempting to produce one for years. When the vaccine arrived and was disseminated, people were still getting ill from the virus. However, death was routed. These effects increased as second vaccinations and booster shots rolled out. As people's immune systems were strengthened, the virus began to wane, and fewer vulnerable hosts were available to infect; diffusion was radically reduced and is now on the way to being controlled—if not eliminated.

The pandemic taught us some timely lessons about the modern world, its conveniences, speed, and the expectations of people living in it. We learned from the virus that our supply chains are fragile. We learned that while viruses move quickly, science does not. Once a virus has taken hold, eradicating it is a long, painful procedure.

The energy of Oturopon works in precisely the same way. It identifies solutions to illness. But in the energy's negative aspect, the disease is used as a cleansing tool, so Oturopon, like the disease itself, is a double-edged sword. It bears diseases into the world, teaching us how to defend ourselves against them.

And that defense system is the complex of learning available to Ifá believers. When the Ashé is fed by wisdom and expressed in the power of the word, the body is fortified. Because, as mentioned earlier, the mind and body—like everything else that exists—are one thing. There is nobody without the mind, and without the body, what is there for the mind to do? What does it interact with?

Thus, how does the Ori exist? Or the Ashé? How does our power proceed to the next life without the flesh? Simply, the Ori and Ashé are Olodumare in us. Personalized to the individual, yet the raw stuff of Divinity, these aspects of being human in the Ifá model are to be recycled, reused, and reimagined as they move through time. Developed for and by us—and our interactions with the wisdom of the word—the Ori and Ashé are subject to evolution as everything else in the cosmology of this religion is. And because they proceed from Olodumare as gifts, they continue in the service of Olodumare as our cycles turn, and these tiny shards of destiny and personal power continue to their next adventure. As they do, their learning continues, feeding Creation with the distant God's now recycled, eternal gifts.

The framing of destiny and power as gifts of God, bestowed and thus intended to serve God, frees them to proceed into eternity. In each cycle of its material existence, the body has transformed with the mind to accomplish the simultaneous unfolding of destiny. It is not obsolete, so much as needed to feed the earth as the Ori and Ashé proceed on their eternal journey.

Self-Defense Is the Power of the Word

Oturopon both bears to us and cures us of disease. Infectious physical diseases are just the start because the greatest diseases humanity is prone to are diseases of the mind: Vanity, rage, deceit, self-obsession, and hatred are only some of them. In the power of the word, these diseases are dispatched from the mind. However, our spiritual and intellectual immune systems are strengthened as they are. The Ashé grows in the human organism unencumbered by disease. When Ashé is strong, the body is strong because the mind is strong.

By creating disease and proposing the solution to feeding the Ashé, Oturopon confronts us with reality. We are creatures of Olodumare, and as creatures, we are well-served by the practice of divination, in which we discover our personal power—the ultimate defense against the ills that human life falls prey to. The power of a human being reinforced with the ancestors' wisdom is difficult to breach. It is also exemplary, presenting the community with the power of the word infused with wisdom.

Ika and Oturopon have a dynamic message about the nature of being human holistically and mindfully. The threats we fear are the threats we must prepare ourselves for every day of our lives. They are neither distant nor near. These threats are a potential awaiting opportunity. We defend ourselves against them through the practice of accumulating and acting upon wisdom to the benefit of mind and body as one integrated reality.

Defending against threats to the organism's health is a function of divination, which has the power to shift destiny. Ika defends, while Oturopon reminds believers why defense is an imperative. The wisdom of the powerful, word-infused Aché, reflecting Olodumare, reflects the ancestors' wisdom serving that God. This is the raw, Divine power that created all. In the human organism, it can serve, or it can flounder. In service, it stands as an imago dei (image of the Divine), showing forth the strength of generations of wisdom that pervades every cell and structure of the follower whose personal power is rooted in the word.

In divination, the supplicant's life is connected to the life of the ancestors and the spirit world. With the mediating word of Odù Ifá reaching across time—and across the two halves of the cosmic gourd—a cure to the diseases of humanity is found. The true Aché's power is reinforced, and the supplicant is freed to live in the intended destiny of the Ori.

The word that reaches out to humanity in divination for the ordering of life and the realization of destiny contains the healing humans seek. Every level of healing is evident here, in body/mind, in community, and between humans and the spirit world. Ika's call to develop personal power in the word is intrinsic to this oral tradition. The oral tradition at the center of Ifá is encapsulated in this demand for power to be lived out in the word of wisdom as the expression of Aché that is most attuned to its source—Olodumare.

Next, we move on to the last part of Odù Ifá covered in this book. While we are only skimming the surface here and providing information for the sake of interest, hopefully, you continue seeking. The Ifá Faith, as you have seen, is complex and sophisticated. It is worth a much deeper exploration than the one offered in these pages.

Chapter 12: Odù Ifá IV — Otura, Irete, Ose, and Ofun

Our final chapter about the Odù Ifá contains the four Odu of Part IV. As explained at the start of Chapter Six, these four Odu are less complex—especially after absorbing many valuable narratives from the Odù Ifá in previous chapters.

Otura

In the world of Otura, comfort is the ability to view everything through the lens of mysticism. This unique type of vision represents the follower finding their way to Olodumare by sharing in the Divine vision.

The root of mysticism is the Ori, and the foundation of the Ori, fully integrated and groomed for eternity, is Otura. Otura is the follower's purpose and destiny. When these are aligned with those of Olodumare, the follower of Ifá is in sync with their intended purpose.

The negative side of Otura is directing the Ori toward the wrong identification, which usually manifests as extreme identification with a group outside the framework of Ifá. Nationalism, racism, and narcissistic self-obsession (extreme identification with the self above all) are examples of mistaken and corrosive identification in Otura.

Mysticism is the comfort of belonging to something immaterial. It is the embrace of the supernatural world, guiding the individual toward the unseen, as a mother hen guides its chicks to the coop.

Derived from the Greek word *mysterion*, meaning "secret ritual or belief," this word is a derivative of the Greek *mystes*, meaning "novice." The root of *mystes* is *muen*, which means to "close" (referring to the mouth/eyes). The implication is that mysticism is a process that is both internal and independent of the physical senses. Mysticism is not pursued by discussions or seeing, or learning; mysticism is experienced at the core of the human being who aligns with the Holy Source.

Mysticism seeks a fundamental connection of the human being to the Source of all that is. Part of that connection is its personal, intimate nature, creating a very specific variety of embraces shared between the human mystic and the Divine Source. This connection is union, and the union is the nature of the Ifá religion, advancing the notion that everything residing in either half of the cosmic gourd resides in the unity of purpose and spirit.

Irete

Irete is like a winepress. From life, it presses the stroke of luck; we all need to have successful lives. However, there is more to Irete than the provision of good fortune. Irete is about determination because determination is what it takes to arrive at the abundance we all desire in life. Determination is required to transform oneself according to the urgings of the Ori and the work of divination. Comforted by the mysticism of Otura, the follower can discern the way forward and leverage determination with the support of divination, guiding and leading with the wisdom of the Odù Ifá.

Irete is bullheaded, demanding that the follower of Ifá hang on to the destiny they have been given and grow it into reality. However, that bullheaded determination can have a negative flip side. That same quality can be misdirected, leading the follower astray with goals that are not tied to their destiny. Worse still, that stubbornness can be negatively transformed into a refusal to change and improve.

Stubbornness has a negative reputation, but it has a purpose. That purpose is not to be stuck in a self stunted by a bullheaded refusal to move forward, change, and grow to come to the full stature of what it means to be a human being practicing Ifá. Irete's purpose is to birth in the follower of Ifá the stubbornness to not give up on themselves or on Olodumare and the Orisha, who represent the distant God.

With the mysticism of Otura influencing the follower, Irete grows into the kind of stubbornness that realizes earthly dreams and builds the Ori for its journey through eternity and its purpose. The two are intimately connected, with mysticism guiding the believer toward their destiny in the spirit world and Irete guiding the believer on earth because on earth, as material beings, we create the template of the Ori's eternity, improving the lives of those around us and growing to be the example others follow.

Ose

The Odu/archetype of Ose is primarily concerned with creating abundance. While Irete teaches and guides the follower to be steadfast in their pursuit of abundance, Ose's underpinnings are in the world and its power. It goes further than Ika (Chapter Eleven) in that it specifically refers to prayer and the use of the word as its basis.

Ose also refers to reproduction and the realization of Irosun (menstrual blood and the womb). Children, in Ifá, are a manifestation of abundance and the materialization of the promise of Irosun. While Irosun refers to all abundance, Ose is more specific in its intentions, directly confronting followers with the imperative to be "fruitful and multiply."

In the world of Ose, abundance and fertility are in the word itself, expressed in prayer. And human sexuality is, naturally, a huge part of that process. The erotic is celebrated and uplifted in Ose, taking pride of place as a key source of human abundance. However, this is not the eroticism of the sex-addled West; this is the eroticism of the desire for children, the erotic playing a key part in the gift of reproduction. Desire is at the heart of Ose, but it is a desire that sees its ultimate end in procreative abundance.

Without humanity's erotic desire, Ose is mocked, and children are not produced, and so, the erotic is canonized in the practice of Ifá in this Odu/archetype. United with Otura's soul-comforting, Ori-growing mysticism, and Irete's squeezing out of life's goodness, Ose conquers by creating abundance that speaks of the family's success, the couple's ardor, and love for one another, and the loving unity of the distant God's Creation.

Lastly, the power of the word is like the abundance of water, causing new life to spring forth. When poured out in prayer, Ose pours abundance on the people. The wisdom-informed word becomes the source of abundance as a manifestation of Olodumare's will, delivering the blessings always intended for humanity, including progeny.

Ofun

Ofun is light. This is the light by which the material world is seen and experienced. Everything you see is seen under the light of Ofun. That is not to say that Ofun is analogous, energetically, to Olodumare. Ofun is an Odu/archetype, energetically acting on the will of Olodumare.

This Odu/archetype is the light of the material world, causing miracles to occur but only by the power of the word. Ika and Ose conspire in Ofun to shine a light on what's stagnant—in need of transformation and regeneration. When the wisdom-informed word is spoken, Ofun reveals the light in the form of miracles.

Answered prayer is Ofun's work in creation, fleshing the power of the word with a response. That response may not be the miracle we envisioned, but it is a miracle. It's in keeping up with destiny, giving us what we needed but which we might not have asked for. We might not have asked for anything, yet the miraculous touches us.

In Ofun, the word's power is ignited, creating a two-way communicative dynamic. The believer calls out to Creation with the word, and Ofun shines the light that reveals the miracle, creating something new.

Interplay and Realization

This final chapter is not unlike a summation of the Principle Odus of Odù Ifá. These four Odu represent the interplay and realization of all the preceding Odu, encompassing the promise of divination for supplicants who come to the priest for guidance and wisdom.

Otura's mysticism pierces the believer, tethering them to the spirit world. Mysticism's leading hand is unseen, immaterial, and known only to the believer. This direct experience of the Divine is unavailable as a shared experience. It exists only in the believer's heart, experiencing God as God is. From this profound place of communion, Irete is born, bringing forth the goodness of the Created Order through the bullheaded determination of the believer. Abundance results but as a gift of the believer to God. It is the efforts of the believer that create abundance. The abundance of Irete is not just a gift; it results from unity with all that is and the actions that proceed due to that unity. Those actions are steadfast and dedicated, never wavering from their objectives. In Ose, the power of the word is the font of procreation and the eroticism which leads to it, realizing the promise of Irosun's womb and menstrual blood. Children are Ose's version of abundance and the manifestation of Irosun. Ofun sheds light on Creation's true form, resulting in miracles as the answer to the wisdom-infused word in prayer.

These four Odu speak to the entire deposit of ancestral knowledge represented by the Odù Ifá as the refined sum of the principal Odu we have read. Every parable, narrative, and poem included in this collection of life lessons hinges on the contents of the sixteen Odu.

The themes of abundance, procreation, and miracles in response to prayer stand as a capsule version of what life is intended to be like in the Ifá cosmology. When humanity has been rightly ordered by orthopraxis, the legacy of that ordering is wrapped in mysticism that leads to abundance. Embodied by the human voice invoking the word in prayer, the light of Ofun pours out on Creation the miracles possible for humanity aligned with the original vision of Olodumare.

The work of eternity is performed when you live, think, and act as a co-creative element in Creation. The cosmic gourd's two halves draw closer together, and God is near again. While Olodumare may not be "just down the block," God is no longer quite so distant, as humanity keeps its part of the bargain.

The Fruit

In these four, Odu is the form of the divine plan for humanity, laid out as a challenge. Humanity has the power to realize the dream of Olodumare: That the cosmic gourd is again whole as one thing, undivided by the grossness of humanity's cavalier behavior.

In learning not to toss our apple cores on God's lawn, we rise to the intended stature of the forms first breathed into by Olodumare as fashioned by Obatala. That dream is one of unity and right action, flowing from the lessons learned in divination, the core of Ifá practice and life. In the Odù Ifá, the guiding lessons and tales of the ancestors draw humanity a picture: This is how human beings should be; this is how they think and behave because this is how the ancestors responded to the challenges and opportunities of life.

The practicality of Ifá is a framework for its mysticism and the promise of an eternity spent recycling, renewing, and reusing the stuff of Creation, just as Olodumare did at the Creative Moment. From the swampy land, Obatala created better earth. It was not a trick with mirrors but a construction project that built a better Creation from existing matter. Today, that project continues in the work of the people of Olodumare, the Ifá, in a religious lifestyle and philosophy of life intended to benefit not just themselves but every living thing.

Without beginning or end, time moves in a circle lived out in human life and the spirit world as a continual and persistent revolution. Refining and bending, pressing and praying, learning, and teaching, the people of Ifá, live their co-creative role in the world as a lifestyle that has persisted for 8,000 years. The next 8,000 years and the years following are not promised, but the Ifá know that time's cycles are set to revolve. And revolve they will, eternally and without cessation.

Conclusion

Your journey into the heart of one of the world's oldest and most sophisticated religions is just starting. Hopefully, this book left you wanting to learn more about Ifá and has encouraged you to continue exploring this ancient religious system and its message to humanity. That message is yours to formulate for yourself. However, at its core, it is a message of working with God to form and reform Creation until it aligns with the vision of Olodumare.

Human beings are given a lofty goal in Ifá, building with the Great Architect the best version of themselves to build one of the best versions of Creation possible. Imagine what a difference that thought might make to the world if we were all to take it to heart.

May your journey continue, and may you know peace and harmony in this life and those that follow.

Here's another book by Mari Silva that you might like

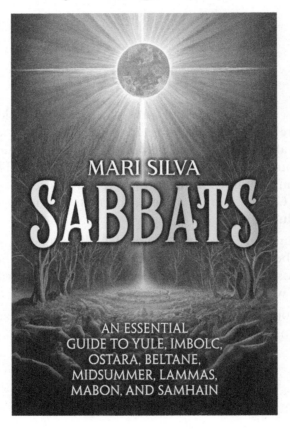

Your Free Gift
(only available for a limited time)

Thanks for getting this book! If you want to learn more about various spirituality topics, then join Mari Silva's community and get a free guided meditation MP3 for awakening your third eye. This guided meditation mp3 is designed to open and strengthen ones third eye so you can experience a higher state of consciousness. Simply visit the link below the image to get started.

https://spiritualityspot.com/meditation

References

15 facts on African religions. (2014, May 16). https://blog.oup.com/2014/05/15-facts-on-african-religions/

Google Arts & Culture. (n.d.). Yoruba people of west Africa. Google Arts & Culture website: https://artsandculture.google.com/usergallery/EQKyzgLnW1j4IQ

Sawe, B. E. (2019, April 17). What is the Yoruba religion? Yoruba beliefs and origin. WorldAtlas website: https://www.worldatlas.com/articles/what-is-the-yoruba-religion.html

Yoruba Religion. (n.d.). Encyclopedia.com website:
https://www.encyclopedia.com/environment/encyclopedias-almanacs-transcripts-and-maps/yoruba-religion

Rodríguez, C. (2020, August 11). Who are Olofin Olorun and Olodumare? Ashé pa mi Cuba. https://ashepamicuba.com/en/quienes-son-olofin-olorun-y-olodumare

Wigington, P. (n.d.). Yoruba religion: History and beliefs. Learn Religions. https://www.learnreligions.com/yoruba-religion-4777660

Cuba, A. pa mi. (2020, July 9). What is an Ebbó? Types and Meanings of this Sacred Astral Cleansing. Ashé pa mi Cuba. https://ashepamicuba.com/en/que-es-un-ebbo-tipos-y-significado

Religion. (n.d.). Jrank.Org. https://science.jrank.org/pages/11051/Religion-African-Diaspora-Spiritual-Assets-Ase-Konesans.html

Rodríguez, C. (2020a, August 1). What is Irunmole? The rise of the Orisha. Ashé pa mi Cuba. https://ashepamicuba.com/en/que-es-irunmole-el-surgimiento-del-orisha

Rodríguez, C. (2020b, August 25). Is there a difference between Orisha and Irunmole? Ashé pa mi Cuba. https://ashepamicuba.com/en/diferencia-entre-orisha-e-irunmole

Who are the Orishas? (2016, September 20). DJONIBA Dance Center. https://www.djoniba.com/who-are-the-orishas

Wigington, P. (n.d.). Yoruba religion: History and beliefs. Learn Religions. https://www.learnreligions.com/yoruba-religion-4777660

Abata – occult world. (n.d.). Occult-World.Com. https://occult-world.com/abata

Ancient Code Team. (2014, December 16). Goddesses Of Yoruba Mythology. Ancient Code. https://www.ancient-code.com/goddesses-yoruba-mythology

Asterope. (n.d.). Deity of the Week. Blogspot.Com. https://deity-of-the-week.blogspot.com/search?q=ayao

Ayao – occult world. (n.d.). Occult-World.Com. https://occult-world.com/ayao

Deities of the Yoruba and Fon Religions. (n.d.). Encyclopedia.Com. https://www.encyclopedia.com/history/news-wires-white-papers-and-books/deities-yoruba-and-fon-religions

Fernández, N. C. (2020, September 12). The Orisha Abata, the entwined Serpent that complements Inle. Ashé pa mi Cuba. https://ashepamicuba.com/en/abata-orisha

Francisca, U. (2020, December 22). See why Olokun is the owner of the deep sea. XoticBrands Home Decor. https://www.xoticbrands.net/blogs/news/olokun

Goddess Oba. (2012, February 26). Journeying to the Goddess. https://journeyingtothegoddess.wordpress.com/2012/02/26/goddess-oba

Iwalaiye, T. (2021, October 22). African Gods: Who is the goddess, Oya? Pulse Nigeria. https://www.pulse.ng/lifestyle/food-travel/african-gods-who-is-the-goddess-oya/q5gf7h2

Konkwo, R. (2018, June 18). Yoruba Gods and Goddesses. Legit.Ng – Nigeria News. https://www.legit.ng/1175618-yoruba-gods-goddesses.html

Nana buruku – occult world. (n.d.). Occult-World.Com. https://occult-world.com/nana-buruku

Rodríguez, C. (2020, October 13). Who is Aha? The Orisha of the Whirlwind and the Wild Wind. Ashé pa mi Cuba. https://ashepamicuba.com/en/orisha-aja

Thafeng, V. A. P. by. (2021, September 6). The mythical origins of the African Goddesses in West African societies. Yoair Blog. https://www.yoair.com/blog/the-mythical-origins-of-the-african-goddesses-in-west-african-societies

Timesofindia. (2021, January 22). Inspiring goddesses from mythology. Times of India. https://timesofindia.indiatimes.com/life-style/books/web-stories/inspiring-goddesses-from-mythology/photostory/80407777.cms

Visit profile. (2012, August 25). West African god and goddess (2). Blogspot.Com. https://kwekudee-tripdownmemorylane.blogspot.com/2012/08/sculptured-impression-of-olorun-1_25.html

Walker, S. (2021, April 27). The ancient beliefs of African goddesses. Amplify Africa. https://www.amplifyafrica.org/post/the-ancient-beliefs-of-african-goddesses

Yewa – Yoruba Goddess of virginity and death. (2021, October 26). Symbol Sage. https://symbolsage.com/yewa-goddess-of-death

About: Erinlẹ. (n.d.). DBpedia. https://dbpedia.org/page/Erinl%E1%BA%B9

Adoga, J., & Gbolahan, A. (2020). Oduduwa. Lulu.com.

Aganju. (n.d.). Gods & Goddess Wiki. https://gods-goddess.fandom.com/wiki/Aganju

Aganju: The deified 4th Alaafin of Oyo. (2019, September 27). WELCOME TO MY WOVEN WORDS. https://mywovenwords.com/2019/09/aganju-the-deified-4th-alaafin-of-oyo.html

Canizares, R., & Lerner, A. E. (2000a). Babalu aye: Santeria and the lord of pestilence. Original Publications.

Canizares, R., & Lerner, A. E. (2000b). Babalu aye: Santeria and the lord of pestilence. Original Publications.

Dennett, R. E. (2019). Eshu. In Nigerian Studies (pp. 94–96). Routledge.

Erinle – occult world. (n.d.). Occult-World.Com. https://occult-world.com/erinle

Joiner-Siedlak, M. (2018, December 17). Babalu Aye – the god of diseases. Monique Joiner Siedlak. https://mojosiedlak.com/babalu-aye-god-diseases

Joiner-Siedlak, M. (2019, September 27). The sacred twins – Ibeji. Monique Joiner Siedlak. https://mojosiedlak.com/the-sacred-twins-ibeji

Konkwo, R. (2018, June 18). Yoruba Gods and Goddesses. Legit.Ng – Nigeria News. https://www.legit.ng/1175618-yoruba-gods-goddesses.html

Mark, J. J. (2021). Orisha. World History Encyclopedia. https://www.worldhistory.org/Orisha

Nut_Meg. (n.d.). Erinle. Obsidianportal.Com. https://god-touched.obsidianportal.com/characters/erinle

Rodríguez, C. (2021, January 5). 10 elements about Oduduwá: Deity who rules the secrets of death. Ashé pa mi Cuba. https://ashepamicuba.com/en/oduduwa-caracteristicas

Ṣàngó. (n.d.). Afropeans.Com. https://afropeans.com/kitchen/%E1%B9%A3ango-yoruba-god-of-thunder

The 5 most influential orishas. (2019, August 11). The Guardian Nigeria News – Nigeria and

World News. https://guardian.ng/life/the-5-most-influential-orishas

The Editors of Encyclopedia Britannica. (2015). Eshu. In Encyclopedia Britannica.

Curnow, K. (n.d.). Chapter 3.6: Art and divination. In The Bright Continent: African Art History. Msl Academic Endeavors.

Divination techniques. (n.d.). Uiowa.edu website: https://africa.uima.uiowa.edu/chapters/divination/divination-techniques/?start=1

Santo, D. E. (2019). Divination. Cambridge Encyclopedia of Anthropology. https://www.anthroencyclopedia.com/entry/divination

Ost, B. (2021). LibGuides: African traditional religions textbook: Ifa: Chapter 5. Our ancestors are with us now. https://research.auctr.edu/c.php?g=1122253&p=8185273

Egun / The ancestors – The Yoruba Religious Concepts. (n.d.). Google.com website: https://sites.google.com/site/theyorubareligiousconcepts/egungun-the-ancestors

Contributed by Kalila Borghini, L. (2010, June 9). Offerings and sacrifices: Honoring our ancestors helps us give thanks. GoodTherapy.org Therapy Blog website:

https://www.goodtherapy.org/blog/offerings

The new exhibit pushes viewers to connect with an African tradition of honoring ancestors. (n.d.). Wisc.edu website: https://news.wisc.edu/new-exhibit-pushes-viewers-to-connect-with-an-african-tradition-of-honoring-ancestors

Cuba, A. pa mi. (2021, February 11). The Orishas, their Syncretism, and Yoruba Calendar of celebrations. Ashé pa mi Cuba. https://ashepamicuba.com/en/calendario-yoruba

Editors. (2021, December 10). Yoruba New Year. New York Latin Culture MagazineTM. https://www.newyorklatinculture.com/yoruba-new-year

Ifa Orisha Egbe Ile Tiwalade Yoruba Community of Metro Atlanta, Georgia. (n.d.). Egbe Tiwalade. http://egbetiwalade.weebly.com/yoruba-calendar.html

Kim, A. (n.d.). How does the Yoruba calendar work? – Theburningofrome.com.

Theburningofrome.Com. https://www.theburningofrome.com/trending/how-does-the-yoruba-calendar-work

Olawale, J. (2018, January 5). Yoruba festivals and holidays in Nigeria. Legit.Ng – Nigeria News. https://www.legit.ng/1143388-yoruba-festivals-holidays-nigeria.html

Oro: A Yoruba festival that is anti-women. (2018, May 7). The Guardian Nigeria News – Nigeria and World News. https://guardian.ng/life/oro-a-yoruba-festival-that-is-anti-women

RajKumar. (2021a, April 16). Months of the year in Yoruba. Happy Days 365. https://happydays365.org/months-of-the-year/months-in-yoruba

RajKumar. (2021b, June 18). Days of the Week in Yoruba. Happy Days 365. https://happydays365.org/days-of-the-week/weekdays-in-yoruba

Surhone, L. M., Timpledon, M. T., & Marseken, S. F. (Eds.). (2010). Yoruba Calendar. Betascript Publishing.

The Centenary Project. (n.d.). New yam festival: A celebration of life and culture. Google Arts & Culture. https://artsandculture.google.com/story/new-yam-festival-a-celebration-of-life-and-culture-pan-atlantic-university/vgUhxQmEwWsNLQ?hl=en

Babalola, A. B., Ogunfolakan, A., & Lababidi, L. (2020, October 29). Rituals, Religious practices, and glass/glass bead making in Ile-Ife and Bida, Nigeria. Endangered Material Knowledge Programme. https://www.emkp.org/rituals-religious-practices-and-glass-glass-bead-making-in-ile-ife-and-bida-nigeria

How to invoke the energy of yorube goddess Oshun. (n.d.). Vice.Com. https://www.vice.com/en/article/3kjepv/how-to-invoke-oshun-yoruba-goddess-orisha

mythictreasures. (2020, May 10). Introduction to 7 day candles. Mythictreasures. https://www.mythictreasures.com/post/into-to-7-day-candles

Urošević, A. (2015, September 23). Spiritual cleansing in Ifá: "sour" and "sweet" baths. Amor et Mortem. https://amoretmortem.wordpress.com/2015/09/23/spiritual-cleansing-in-Ifa-sour-and-sweet-baths

Brandon, G. (2018). orisha. In Encyclopedia Britannica.

"Santeria": La Regla de Ocha-Ifa and lukumi. (n.d.). Pluralism.org website: https://pluralism.org/%E2%80%9Csanter%C3%ADa%E2%80%9D-the-lucumi-way

Dialogue Institute. (n.d.). Afro-Caribbean and African religion information —.Dialogue Institute website: https://dialogueinstitute.org/afrocaribbean-and-african-religion-information

Currents Staff. (n.d.). African-based religions: Santeria, Candomble, vodoun. Riverwestcurrents.org website: https://riverwestcurrents.org/2006/04/african-based-religions-santeria-candomble-vodoun.html

Aganyu – occult world. (n.d.). Occult-world.com website: https://occult-world.com/aganyu

Ajé-shaluga – occult world. (n.d.). Occult-world.com website: https://occult-world.com/aje-shaluga

Asterope. (n.d.). Deity of the Week. Blogspot.com website: http://deity-of-the-week.blogspot.com/search/label/yoruban

Ayao – occult world. (n.d.). Occult-world.com website: https://occult-world.com/ayao

Babalu ayé – occult world. (n.d.). Occult-world.com website: https://occult-world.com/babalu-aye

Coburg, A. (2012). Osain: Cantos a osain (1st ed.). http://readersandrootworkers.org/wiki/Osain

Eshu elegbara – occult world. (n.d.). Occult-world.com website: https://occult-world.com/eshu-elegbara

evelynna. (n.d.). Oxumaré written by Evelynn Amabeoku. Blogspot.com website: http://ucrpandas.blogspot.com/2009/05/oxumare-written-by-evelynn-amabeoku.html

Fatunmbi, L. (2000). Ochosi: IFA and the spirit of the tracker. Plainview, NY: Original
Publications.

Fatunmbi, L., & Canizares, R. (2000). Obatala: Santeria and the white-robed king of the Orisha. Plainview, NY: Original Publications.

Fernández, N. C. (2020, December 11). Do you know the Sacred Herbs of Oshosi? 8 Plants you should know. Ashé pa mi Cuba website: https://ashepamicuba.com/en/hierbas-de-oshosi

Fernández, N. C. (2021, January 10). Ayana, Aja, and Ayao: Three very powerful minor deities of the Osha. Ashé pa mi Cuba website: https://ashepamicuba.com/en/ayana-aja-y-ayao

Goddess Egungun-Oya. (2012, June 6). Journeying to the Goddess website: https://journeyingtothegoddess.wordpress.com/2012/06/06/goddess-egungun-oya

Ibeji – occult world. (n.d.). Occult-world.com website: https://occult-world.com/ibeji

Joiner-Siedlak, M. (2019, June 6). Ochosi – the Hunter. Monique Joiner Siedlak website:
https://mojosiedlak.com/ochosi-the-hunter

Mark, J. J. (2021). Orisha. World History Encyclopedia.
https://www.worldhistory.org/Orisha

Mawu mother earth. (2013, August 27). Moon Mothers of Half Moon Bay website:

Mawu-Lisa – occult world. (n.d.). Occult-world.com website: https://occult-world.com/mawu-lisa

"Mawu's themes are creativity, Universal Law, passion, abundance, birth, and inspiration. Her symbols are clay and …. (n.d.). Pinterest website:
https://www.pinterest.com/pin/542543704955561047

Melissa. (2018, March 17). Oshumare – the sacred serpent. Afro-diasporic Religiosity website:
https://candombleusa.wordpress.com/2018/03/17/oshumare-the-sacred-serpent

Nana buruku – occult world. (n.d.). Occult-world.com website: https://occult-world.com/nana-buruku

Oba – occult world. (n.d.). Occult-world.com website: https://occult-world.com/oba

Ogun. (n.d.). Santeria Church of the Orishas website:
http://santeriachurch.org/the-orishas/ogun

Ogun – occult world. (n.d.). Occult-world.com website: https://occult-world.com/ogun

OLODUMARE – the Yoruba Religious concepts. (n.d.). Google.com website:
https://sites.google.com/site/theyorubareligiousconcepts/olodumare

Olokun – occult world. (n.d.). Occult-world.com website: https://occult-world.com/olokun

Orisha – occult world. (n.d.). Occult-world.com website: https://occult-world.com/orisha

Orisha Oko. (n.d.). Santeria Church of the Orishas website:
http://santeriachurch.org/the-orishas/orisha-oko

Orisha oko – occult world. (n.d.). Occult-world.com website: https://occult-world.com/orisha-oko

Osain – occult world. (n.d.). Occult-world.com website: https://occult-world.com/osain

Oshumare – occult world. (n.d.). Occult-world.com website: https://occult-world.com/oshumare

Oshun – occult world. (n.d.). Occult-world.com website: https://occult-world.com/oshun

Oya – occult world. (n.d.). Occult-world.com website: https://occult-world.com/oya

Purple Moon – Orisha Osain. (n.d.). Pmtarot.com website:
https://www.pmtarot.com/m/showproduct.php?p=07278&c=&lang=eng

Rodríguez, C. (2020a, August 24). SUBSCRIBE FOR FREE Eleguá is the Orisha eternal guardian of the roads and Read more. Ashé pa mi Cuba website: https://ashepamicuba.com/en/plantas-de-elegua

Rodríguez, C. (2020b, August 27). 10 representative plants of Obatalá. Ashé pa mi Cuba website: https://ashepamicuba.com/en/plantas-de-obatala

Rodríguez, C. (2021, January 5). 10 elements about Oduduwá: Deity who rules the secrets of death. Ashé pa mi Cuba website: https://ashepamicuba.com/en/oduduwa-caracteristicas

SAGE reference – encyclopedia of African religion. (n.d.). Sagepub.com website: https://sk.sagepub.com/reference/africanreligion/n323.xml

templeofathena. (2016, September 9). GMC: Orisha Osumare. Temple of Athena the Savior website: https://templeofathena.wordpress.com/2016/09/09/gmc-orisha-osumare

The Afro-Cuban Orisha pantheon. (n.d.). Historymiami.org website:

Vaughan, S. A. (2017). Ibeji. http://santeriachurch.org/the-orishas/ibeji /

Visit profile. (2013, December 11). Olokun deity and its various olokun festivals. Blogspot.com website: https://kwekudee-tripdownmemorylane.blogspot.com/2013/12/olokun-deity-and-its-various-olokun.html

Yemaya – occult world. (n.d.). Occult-world.com website: https://occult-world.com/yemaya

AfrikaIsWoke.Com. *Ifa oracle: The 16 Odu Ifa & their meaning.* (2022, February 3). https://www.afrikaiswoke.com/ifa-oracle-the-16-odu-ifa-their-meaning/

Atlanta University Center Woodruff Library. (2022). *African traditional religions: Ifa.* Atla. https://atla.libguides.com/c.php?g=1138564&p=8386152

Bascom, W. R. (1969). *Ifa divination: Communication between gods and men in West Africa.* Indiana University Press.

Dev, B. (2016, February 4). *Eight interesting facts about the Yoruba people.* Bashiri. https://bashiri.com.au/eight-interesting-facts-yoruba-people/

Faseyin, A. Z., & Faseyin, F. A. Y. (2006). *IWAKERI: The quest for Afrikan spirituality by Awotunde Yao Zannu Faseyin.* Lulu Enterprises Incorporated.

Harvard University. (n.d.). *Ifa.* https://projects.iq.harvard.edu/predictionx/ifa

Odutola, K. (2019. *Yoruba culture & customs.* Ufl.Edu.

Packer, M. J., & Tibaduiza Sierra, S. (2012). A concrete psychological investigation of ifá divination. *Revista Colombiana de Psicología, 21*(2), 355–371.

Study.Com. *Yoruba people: Language, culture & music.* (n.d.). https://study.com/academy/lesson/yoruba-people-language-culture-music.html

Walker, R. A. (2009). *The arts of Africa at the Dallas Museum of Art.* Yale University Press.

Winn, L. M., & Jacknis, I. (Eds.). (2004.). *Yoruba art & culture.* University of California. https://hearstmuseum.berkeley.edu/wp-content/uploads/TeachingKit_YorubaArtAndCulture.pdf

Made in the USA
Las Vegas, NV
30 November 2023